Historic WINTERSBURG IN HUNTINGTON BEACH

Historic WINTERSBURG IN HUNTINGTON BEACH

Mary F. Adams Urashima

THE
History
PRESS

Published by The History Press
Charleston, SC 29403
www.historypress.net

Front cover, top left: Charles Mitsuji Furuta and Yukiko Yajima Furuta with son Raymond, circa 1915. *Furuta family collection*; *top center*: Yukiko Yajima Furuta at the Long Beach Pike in Southern California, circa 1913. *Furuta family collection*; *top right*: Charles Mitsuji Furuta hauling hay, most likely at the Cole Ranch in Wintersburg Village, circa 1911. *Furuta family collection*; *bottom center*: Charles Mitsuji Furuta with an unknown man in a Wintersburg Village–area celery field, circa 1912–14. *Furuta family collection.*
Back cover, top: Etsuko, Kazuko, Nobuko, Toshiko and Raymond Furuta next to the Furuta bungalow in Wintersburg Village, taken on January 10, 1926. *Furuta family collection*; *inset*: Toshiko and Raymond Furuta with Sumi Akiyama at the Cole Ranch in Wintersburg Village, circa 1918. *Center for Oral and Public History California State University–Fullerton, PJA 288.*

First published 2014

ISBN 9781540222831

Library of Congress CIP data applied for.

For my son, Keane Patrick Yoshio Urashima, in whose eyes I see the future.

CONTENTS

Contents

ACKNOWLEDGEMENTS

I thank my parents, Paul and Barbara Adams, for infusing me with a love of American history—both of our own family history and that of others. The hours spent in family parlors and museums and exploring ruins and historic places were not in vain.

My deep gratitude goes to Norman, Kenneth and Dave Furuta; their mother, Martha Furuta; their aunt, Etsuko Furuta Fukushima; and the extended Furuta family for generously sharing their history as an American pioneer family. Your story is inspiring.

Special thanks to the Wintersburg Presbyterian Church, whose remarkable history as a pioneer mission is deserving of recognition and study.

There are scholars who work endlessly to save this history for future generations, and among them are Professor Emeritus Arthur A. Hansen, whose decades-long effort to record oral histories and research and share Japanese American history is a model for others—thank you for being a mentor; Stephanie George from California State University–Fullerton, Center of Oral and Public History, a generous and patient soul who opened the archives and shared enthusiasm for this history; and Chris Jepsen, with the Orange County Archives, who raised an early alarm about the potential loss of the Historic Wintersburg property, always added encouraging words and tracked down documents and photographs that help tell the stories of Wintersburg Village and Orange County's Japanese community.

Deep gratitude to my friends and Historic Wintersburg Preservation Task Force members, advisors and supporters: Gloria Alvarez, Stacha Khatib,

ACKNOWLEDGEMENTS

Dennis Masuda, Dave Wentworth, Barbara Haynes, Elaine Parker, Phil Chinn, Kanji Sahara, Dann Gibb and Chris Epting. City of Huntington Beach council member and mayor Connie Boardman, thank you for your support and for devoting time to the task force.

The best people are met via historic preservation. Thank you to Tadashi Kowta and the Kowta family; Donna Graves, Preserving California's Japantowns; Asian Pacific Islanders in Historic Preservation; California Preservation Foundation; the Little Tokyo Historical Society; *Lil Tokyo Reporter* cast, producers and crew; Orange County Historical Commission; Huntington Beach Historic Resources Board; Huntington Beach Historical Society; Fountain Valley Historical Society; Manzanar Committee; Discover Nikkei and the Japanese American National Museum; Evelyn Shimazo Yee; Douglas McIntosh; Beth Padon; Jim Vitale; Charles Leik, National Barn Alliance; and the many Huntington Beach residents and organizations that came forward to support preservation of our cultural heritage.

There is always a risk I have neglected to mention someone. Many have wished this effort goodwill. To all who have contributed information, support and an encouraging word, I thank you.

INTRODUCTION

Wintersburg Village was a rural community that developed in the mid- to late 1800s in what is now north Huntington Beach, Orange County, California. Once part of the Rancho la Bolsa Chica—acquired by land baron Abel Stearns—the ranch and peatlands began to be sold off in smaller parcels after the drought of 1863–64.

European American pioneers looking for a new life gravitated to Southern California with the prospect of land ownership, beautiful weather and rich peat soil. Cattle-grazing land was replaced with farms. At the same time, the Meiji era in Japan ended the role of the samurai, prompting economic and social changes that resulted in Japanese pioneers leaving for America.

Meeting in Orange County, these distinct groups created Wintersburg Village in an environment that was still very much the pioneer West, with horse thieves, gun battles, invention, tragedy and triumph and bigger-than-life personalities. Those who risked everything to make California their home embodied the pioneer spirit and had enthusiasm for America's future.

The Wintersburg District became a thriving farm community, with a railroad siding to load produce for market, the Tashima Market for feed and seed, the McIntosh meat store, the Ocean View Grammar School, a Japanese baseball team, three goldfish farms, an armory and two churches—the Methodist Episcopal Church in 1906 and the Wintersburg Japanese Presbyterian Mission in 1910. Wintersburg Village became the heart of the early 1900s Japanese community in coastal Orange County, an integrated village of Japanese and European pioneers.

Japanese pioneers—the *Issei*, or immigrant generation, and the *Nisei*, those born in America—faced the same challenges as all pioneers, surviving by their own physical endurance, tenacity, ingenuity and optimism. In California, they also faced extreme discrimination, which restricted their path to citizenship and land ownership and excluded them from certain professions.

At the same time, in rural Orange County, Japanese immigrants were embraced by many of their neighbors, forming business relationships and friendships that survived difficult times. The establishment of community schools, cultivation of the arts and contribution to civic efforts—such as the rebuilding of the Huntington Beach pier in 1914—speak to the larger community partnership. It is perhaps not a coincidence that the first Japanese American mayor of a continental U.S. city and California's first Supreme Court justice were from Orange County, both having attended the mission in Wintersburg Village.

Historic Wintersburg in Huntington Beach is only a fraction of the history of Orange County's Japanese pioneers. Their imprint on its development and culture is undeniable.

Chapter 1

MR. WINTERS GOES
TO CHICAGO

In 1893, Chicago hosted the World's Columbian Exposition—a 630-acre international World's Fair of extraordinary scope and the subject of a multitude of books and documentaries. Southern California's counties banded together to create a World's Fair Association, joining their exhibits in the Columbian Exposition's California Building. With the exception of the building for the host state of Illinois, the California building was reported as the largest state building on the exposition grounds.

The *Final Report of the California World's Fair Commission* in 1894 remarks:

> *Orange County displayed her citrus and deciduous fruits in such a manner as to bring them prominently before the public. Her exhibit of fruit in glass was among the largest of any of the southern counties, while her output in the agricultural line disclosed a pleasing variety of marketable vegetables and luxuriant grains. Her large beets, squash, celery, cucumbers, corn, oats, etc. attracted much attention, while the specimens of peat soil evoked marked comment.*

The report continues to laud California's agricultural bounty, describing the state as "lavish in her display" and that "an expression frequently heard was: 'If there is any vacant space in the Horticultural Building, California will step to the front and fill it.'"

A large part of the success of the Orange County exhibit had to do with Luther Henry Winters, for whom Wintersburg Village was named.

World's Columbian Exposition grounds, 1893. *Frances Benjamin Johnston Collection, Library of Congress.*

In Samuel Armor's 1921 *History of Orange County*, Winters—originally from Warren, Ohio—is described as "a conspicuous example of a successful agriculturist, and notably associated with the advancement of the county." Armor continues:

> *In the early years of the county's history, Mr. Winters purchased twenty acres of land in Ocean View, where his home is situated in what is now the great celery district. His land yielded 137 bushels of shelled corn and 100 sacks of marketable potatoes to the acre the first year...samples of this remarkable showing were placed on exhibition at the World's Columbian*

World's Columbian Exposition, long boat on Venetian Canal, 1893. *Frances Benjamin Johnston Collection, Library of Congress.*

World's Columbian Exposition, aerial view of exposition grounds, 1893. *Francis Benjamin Johnston Collection Library of Congress.*

World's Columbian Exposition, inside one of the mammoth exhibit halls, 1893. *Hemming Hultgren, U.S. public domain.*

Exposition, in 1893, and created a sensation. Probably this exhibit, more than any other display from California, had a tendency to place the resources of Orange County in the proper light before the world in general.

The opening remarks of James D. Phelan, vice-president of the California World's Fair Commission, acknowledged that California's presence at the fair was not "actuated entirely by sentiment."

"Californians had also other reasons for coming to Chicago," explained Phelan. "We came here to show the part we are playing on the great stage of the world. We came here to show the development of the State since the American occupation in 1846. We came here to enlarge our markets and invite a new immigration."

Phelan also noted an inscription in the California building, "California, esto perpetua," that perplexed a fellow American, who repeated the phrase several times until announcing, "I have it! California is perfect!" Phelan joked that the man then added, "Another California brag."

California, however, made good on its boast.

"Nothing in the whole exhibition even approaches the display made by the Californians," reported *Age*, a paper from Melbourne, Australia, in July 1893.

"California on Admission day [September 9] was making herself felt from one end of the globe to the other. People of all nations, classes and colors rushed for the California Building," reported the *Tribune* from Salt Lake City, Utah, in September 1893.

The same month, the exhibition city's newspaper the *Chicago Herald* reported, "California has fairly outdone all the States, and her big building heaped with barrels of sparkling wine, tons of delicious fruits, grains and vegetables is a never-failing source of delight to exposition sight-seers."

Kate Field's Washington, a correspondent from Washington, D.C., reported that a friend commented, "If I were asked what one word best expresses California, I should answer, 'plenty.' The moment I enter her building, I feel like eating and drinking.'"

The California World's Fair Commission's report includes the transcript of visitor comments about the California exhibit, with remarks such as, "This is the greatest show on earth," "Why can't I go and live there permanently?" "Hurrah for California" and, humorously, "California against the world."

World's Columbian Exposition, Japanese craftsmen working on the Japanese Pavilion, 1893. *Library of Congress.*

California media, like the *Times* from Oakland, reported back home:

People appear to be in a state of excitement as they stand around and descant on the things displayed in the California Building. Everyone seems to want to have a connecting link to California—either they have a relative there or a friend, or have made a visit, or announce that they will never die happy till they have made the trip. It is almost touching to hear the longings and the affection that nearly everyone here seems to have for the State.

Because Winters's name was with the exhibit, he received, according to county historian Armor, "a large correspondence from incredulous and inquiring observers, which he personally answered." Winters—married to Cordelia Wilson, a native-born Californian from Pasadena—returned home and continued to display the agricultural wealth of the Orange County countryside at the Los Angeles Chamber of Commerce and at county fairs.

Winters's successful agricultural ventures and his ambassadorship for Orange County led to his being named the president of the California Celery Company, during which time he placed Orange County celery in eastern U.S. markets. Winters also donated land for the rail line that went through his rural country town and land for other township purposes. Grateful residents circulated a petition to name the town in his honor, officially creating the little community of Wintersburg Village.

Winters built a "beautiful and commodious bungalow in the suburbs of Wintersburg, where he and his family reside and keep up the old time hospitality for which California of olden days was renowned," writes Armor, lauding Winters for keeping a family orchard and vegetable garden "in which he grows fifty varieties of fruits." A California State Mining Bureau map of Huntington Beach–Newport Oil Fields from 1920 locates Henry Winters's property to the west of the Southern Pacific Railroad line, northeast of the present-day intersection of Goldenwest Street and Warner Avenue. His land was north of the Cole Ranch and other local farms, now occupied by the Ocean View High School and a hardware chain store.

Wintersburg Village has faded into the urban hum of Huntington Beach. Henry Winters's name was removed from Wintersburg Avenue (now Warner Avenue). A shopping center, restaurants and a parking lot replaced the farmland on which he grew his renowned produce, which had been the site of a cooperative land venture known as the "Winters Club" in the mid-1920s. The only elements Henry Winters would recognize in his former village today are the 1906 ME Church, the 1910 Wintersburg Japanese Presbyterian Mission and the remaining tracks of the Southern Pacific Railroad's Smeltzer-Wintersburg siding.

Samuel Armor's final comment about pioneer agriculturalist Winters was that "the wealth and success he has wrested from crude but promising materials commend itself to the consideration of the younger generation who may be imbued with ambition and possess the adequate energy and continuity of purpose to surmount the obstacles that lie in the pathway of success." Winters saw opportunity in the peatlands of Orange County and others would follow.

Chapter 2

COMING TO AMERICA

C harles Furuta was eighteen years old when he left the rural countryside of Hiroshima-ken for Hawaii to meet his older brother, Soichi. Their father had died when Charles was five. The politics and economy in Japan were changing, and his family had little land. But at the dawn of 1900, there was work in Hawaii, and his brother would be there. He would not be alone.

When he arrived in Honolulu, the turn of events there forever changed generations of his family.

Black plague was sweeping the islands. Those on ships were not allowed to disembark. The board of health closed the port. Any ships in the harbor were ordered to move away from the dock to avoid rats jumping from land to ship. Schools were closed, lime spread around neighborhoods, armed guards stationed around Chinatown and the working class ordered to stay indoors. Health officials began setting "sanitary fires" in areas where there had been plague symptoms. Chinatown was set on fire, leaving thousands homeless.

Left with no other choice, the British steamer SS *Glenogle* continued to Tacoma, Washington, with Charles Furuta on board. The SS *Glenogle* had "[come] into violent collision" with the *City of Kingston* in Tacoma Harbor only one year earlier and had been taken to court for "total disregard of the rules and laws of navigation in force in the waters of the United States." The captain was accused of speeding into the harbor through heavy fog without signal whistles, crushing the hull of the *City of Kingston*. The *Glenogle* was patched up and, like other steamships of the time, disinfected to kill rats, its passengers' baggage steamed to avoid contagion. There was risk and little luxury in ocean travel. For Charles

Furuta, there was the added uncertainty of venturing on to an unknown country.

Having made it across the Pacific, his first glimpse of America on May 24, 1900, was a northwest harbor crowded with ships, floating logs and a muddy port town bustling with activity. Tacoma was a major crossroads for the railroad and lumber companies. Charles found jobs working at a sawmill and on railroad construction.

Charles Mitsuji Furuta and brother Soichi Furuta (location unknown), January 1904. *Furuta family collection.*

Charles's future wife, Yukiko Yajima—the daughter of a samurai family—was five years old at the time, living in Hiroshima-ken. Although her family had lost wealth and position along with most samurai of the time, her father was successful in the business of selling safes, affording her the opportunity for education.

A childhood memory that stood out for eighty-seven-year-old Yukiko during her 1982 oral history interview was walking across the *Yanagi Bashi*, or "Willow Bridge" on her way to school.

After several years in the cold, damp northwest, Charles decided to leave for Southern California.

Masuko Yajima Akiyama and Yukiko Yajima Furuta, circa 1899, Hiroshima-ken, Japan. *Furuta family collection.*

21

Mr. Kimura and Yukiko Furuta with her mother, Ei Yajima, at Momijidani, Miyajima Island, Hiroshima-ken, circa 1912. *Furuta family collection.*

He had heard that "there were more chances of getting a job and also the weather was good," explained Yukiko. The lure of Southern California had already taken hold in America, with postcard images of citrus groves and miles of beaches.

"He heard about Smeltzer…as the place where celery was being raised and that there would be a lot of jobs here," recalled Yukiko. One more time, Charles Furuta would venture to another destination alone.

LAND OF CELERY

By the time Charles Furuta arrived in Orange County's celery fields, production had grown to the point that twenty-five to thirty carloads of celery left via the Southern Pacific Railroad every day to points around the country. It was just the beginning of the celery boom. Local growers were trying to keep up, hiring the Japanese immigrants who had begun arriving at the turn of the century.

Wintersburg Village, where Charles Furuta ended up making his home, was predominantly flat, open farm land filled with tules, patches of vegetable crops, a few dirt roads and a railroad running straight through it. It was still very much a don't-blink-or-you'll-miss-it collection of buildings. There was a small Japanese population gathering, many of the bachelor workers living in labor camps and traveling to farming areas throughout California.

Tsuneji Chino and wife, circa 1905. Chino managed a large labor camp in Smeltzer and was a supporter of the Wintersburg Mission. *California State University Fullerton, Center for Oral and Public History PJA 512.*

At the labor camps, each landlord provided his laborers with housing. Workers typically slept on blankets on the floor. After the harvest, blankets were rolled up, and workers left for a boardinghouse in Los Angeles's "Little Tokyo" until the next job. Referred to as *buranke-katsugi* or "blanket carriers," the Japanese laborers worked ten hours daily, Monday through Saturday, for about fifteen cents an hour. In northwest Orange County, the known labor camps were located near Warner Avenue and Springdale Street and along Smeltzer (now Edinger) Avenue in present-day Huntington Beach.

When they were able, Japanese farmers leased houses or built temporary homes on leased land.

"The houses that [most] Japanese farmers built were just improvised shacks," explained Clarence Nishizu, a congregant of the Wintersburg Japanese Presbyterian Mission. "They had no building inspectors in those days, so the farmers built houses any way they wanted to, just so that the walls stood up…the wallpaper of the inside walls was newspaper in some of the rooms."

Nishizu explained the reason behind the temporary nature of most of the Japanese community's housing: "Since the farmers leased land and were too poor to buy land, most of them built houses with the intention of moving again. Therefore, the floors were built in sections so that they could easily be dismantled and moved again."

"The wooden shacks we lived in were very cold in wintertime…the walls did not have any insulation whatsoever," Nishizu recalled. "We had to use lots of futon [comforters] during wintertime, and we couldn't wait to get near the stove to dress on cold mornings."

The Japanese were not living all that differently from other pioneers arriving in the peatlands. Tents and temporary housing were common in the

Charles Furuta driving hay wagon on Cole Ranch, Wintersburg, 1911. *Furuta family collection.*

Reverend Terasawa (second from left) with Charles Furuta (second from right), labor camp manager Tsuneji Chino (far left) and unknown man in Wintersburg Village. *Furuta family collection.*

early years, as was moving buildings. However, local residents began to feel the need for permanency.

One of the wooden buildings moved to Wintersburg Village from Talbert was an armory building, placed near the Southern Pacific Railroad line. Walking in off the dusty road and sitting on produce crates, locals held a community meeting in 1904. The small group of farmers and businessmen discussed the need for churches. Since 1902, clergy had been talking to workers in the celery fields and recognized the need for a mission.

Wintersburg goldfish farmer Henry Kiyomi Akiyama remembered in his 1982 oral history interview that some of the *Issei* celery workers in the labor camps spent their Sundays attending church. Cambridge University– educated Reverend Hisakichi Terasawa—a bilingual Episcopalian minister—had begun missionary work among the Japanese community, in partnership with Presbyterian clergy from nearby Westminster. Terasawa used a leased Wintersburg barn to make a gathering place for the Japanese men, mostly bachelors.

Reverend Terasawa was one of the first people Charles Furuta met when arriving in Wintersburg. Terasawa taught him English and introduced Charles to the Christian faith, making him the first Japanese immigrant baptized in Orange County. Just as bubonic plague in Hawaii had diverted Charles to America's mainland, meeting Reverend Terasawa became another turning point.

"He felt as if Reverend Terasawa was his father, and Reverend Terasawa treated him like his son," explained Yukiko Furuta in 1982. He later became like a grandfather to the Furuta children, maintaining a long relationship with the Furuta family.

One of Charles's ventures in his early years in Wintersburg was a farm cooperative with four other Japanese men, referred to as a *goshinsha*, located along what is now Goldenwest Street, south of Bolsa Avenue. Loosely translated, *goshinsha* meant "five working as one." Not successful due to crop failure, the *goshinsha* racked up $10,000 in debt, and the other men disappeared. Furuta continued to work and pay off the debt on his own, while continuing his studies with Terasawa in a Wintersburg barn after working long hours in the fields.

Describing her husband eight decades later during her oral history interview, Yukiko explains he was "a very sincere Christian and an honest, hard-working man. He did not smoke or drink."

"So he got a very good reputation from the *hakujin* [Caucasian] farm owner" from whom he rented land, Yukiko recalled. "He could borrow money from this owner. He worked very hard so he could pay back the debt and even save money to buy the land."

It was Terasawa who advised his Japanese congregants to buy land; Charles Furuta was one of the few who listened. On March 2, 1908, the five-acre parcel off Wintersburg Avenue and Nichols Lane was purchased from John and Forrest Dubois; Wallace Blaylock and Emma Blaylock, his wife; and Ida Caldwell, an unmarried woman, for a recorded ten dollars by Reverend Terasawa, with financial support from Charles Furuta. The deed held at the Orange County archives indicates the property had previously been purchased from the Stearns Rancho Company as part of the former Rancho la Bolsa Chica and included a share in an artesian water well.

By February 28, 1912—months before California passed the Alien Land Law of 1913—Furuta (along with the president of the Japanese mission

Hiroshima-ken, circa 1912, at the time Charles returned to meet Yukiko. *Furuta family collection.*

Yukiko Yajima Furuta with classmates, Hiroshima 1910. *Furuta family collection.*

building committee) bought the farmland from Reverend Terasawa for ten dollars, who deeded the land to them. Terasawa returned to his home in San Francisco to join his wife, Fuku. The majority of the land would become the Furuta farm, the northwest corner set aside for the Wintersburg

Japanese Presbyterian Mission. Charles would later donate more land for the mission's expansion, becoming its largest benefactor and eventually an elder in the church.

After the land purchase in 1912, having worked to eliminate debt from farming ventures with others, and officially a landowner, Charles Furuta was determined to set down permanent roots in America. He planned his first trip back to Japan since his departure in 1900 to meet his future bride.

MEETING YUKIKO

A family friend arranged for Charles to meet Yukiko. Yukiko recalls a neighbor telling her she could have a good life in America, an indication that a potential marriage was being arranged for her. Seventeen at the time, she remembers thinking "that if it was such a nice country, she would go."

Her interpreter in 1982 explains, "One day this lady asked her to go to a public bath house with her…when they finished taking the bath, this lady

Reverend John Junzo Nakamura with Yukiko Yajima Furuta, Tokyo, circa 1912. *Furuta family collection.*

28

Above: Yukiko Yajima Furuta
at Charles Furuta's house,
Hiroshima-ken, Japan, 1912.
Furuta family collection.

Right: Yukiko Yajima Furuta,
1912. *Furuta family collection.*

told Mrs. Furuta, 'Go home before me and if some guests come to your house, please serve them an ashtray and a cigarette set.'" The first meeting was arranged, and two men came to visit. One was the go-between, and the other was thirty-one-year-old American landowner Charles Furuta.

Returning to America on the *Shinyo Maru*, 1912. *Furuta family collection.*

Yukiko and Charles M. Furuta, newly married and starting their life
in Wintersburg Village, circa 1913. *Furuta family collection.*

After a traditional country marriage ceremony, the couple went by train to Yokohama and from there departed for America on the *Shinyo Maru*. Yukiko remembered buying "uncut rolls of sushi from the galley, and how good this sushi was." It took a little over two weeks to reach San Francisco, where they were met by Charles's friend and mentor Reverend Terasawa. His wife, Fuku, took Yukiko to Market Street—already filled with trolleys, cars and "skyscrapers"—for her first Western shopping experience.

Later, arriving in Little Tokyo in Los Angeles, the Furutas stayed at the Miyako Hotel on First Street (renamed the Civic Hotel). In 1912, Little Tokyo was a thriving center for the Japanese immigrant community.

Seven decades later, Yukiko said she had no nervousness or fear in leaving Japan. She was "told by the other people that Mr. Furuta was a very good man. So if she would follow him, there would be nothing to fear and nothing to worry about. So, she trusted him and just came to the United States without any fear at all." In later years, Yukiko told her adult children—when they looked at a photograph taken of her in Tokyo in 1912—that she was nervous and uncertain what life would be like in America. The marriage of Yukiko and Charles Furuta was, ultimately, a love match, lasting forty-one years until Charles's death in 1953.

BUILDING A HOME

While Yukiko remained at the hotel in Little Tokyo, Charles made arrangements for the construction of their home in Wintersburg. Commuting via the Pacific Electric Railway from Los Angeles to Orange County, he was able to get a loan from the Huntington Beach bank with the land as equity. Unusual for the time, he contracted with a Caucasian builder, who also is believed to have constructed the barn on the Furuta farm.

Left on her own while he was working, Yukiko remembered Charles always left her money. Her oral history interpreter described her first days: "She just went to *Fugetsudo*—that was a Japanese confectionary store in Los Angeles— to buy some confections, and came back to the hotel room and ate them." (Fugetsu-do, the 1903 sweet shop, remains today at 315 East First Street in Little Tokyo.) She remembered the few Japanese restaurants in Little Tokyo at that time were very simple, with dirt floors and not to her liking.

Charles waited to show her the land until the home was almost finished. Facing Wintersburg Avenue, the classic California bungalow was prominent

Yukiko Yajima Furuta at Long Beach Pike, California, 1912. *Furuta family collection.*

Yukiko and Charles M. Furuta, in front of new house in Wintersburg, 1912. *Furuta family collection.*

on the farmland, painted a deep iron oxide red with white trim and a small, whitewashed front porch. The land was filled with "gum trees" that Charles had planted to provide wood for cooking and heating the traditional Japanese bath, or *ofuro*, he installed behind the house. He had purchased a new kerosene stove for Yukiko.

The first photographs of them at the house show the final touches being made and the garden yet to be planted. It was one of the few new houses in Wintersburg, considered modern and, Yukiko notes, "at that time...very remarkable" and admired "because other Japanese who owned houses bought old houses."

Yukiko recalled being one of the first Japanese wives in the Wintersburg area and one of the few who did not work in the fields. She spent her first months as a new wife feeling the loneliness of the "vast" pioneer country and trying to learn how to cook and make house from Japanese magazines. Learning English from Charles, Yukiko found it difficult at first to meet and talk with her Caucasian neighbors.

She told her interpreter, "You know, in Japan, mothers-in-law and daughters-in-law did not often have good relationships. It's hard for a daughter-in-law to live with a mother-in-law, because she has to obey the mother-in-law...but she thought that, even if a mother-in-law was not so kind, if she would have a mother-in-law, that would be much better than being so lonely."

Charles was protective, telling her to stay inside and lock the doors when he was away. He put her on the handlebars of his bicycle when they rode around the dirt roads of Wintersburg Village, Yukiko hopping off when they saw people to avoid the embarrassment. Charles also constructed a tennis court on the farm, a sport Yukiko had loved in Japan. His grandchildren jokingly identified an early 1900s photograph of Charles playing tennis with his unique "ambidextrous swing," avoiding a backhand by changing the racket from hand to hand for a forehand swing.

The Furuta farm became a natural gathering place for others in the Japanese community due to the growing activities of the mission on the farm, the Tashima Market across Wintersburg Avenue and the Wintersburg-Smeltzer siding of the Southern Pacific Railroad, where farmers loaded produce.

Most of Charles's and Yukiko's activities revolved around the Wintersburg Japanese Presbyterian Mission. They socialized with the clergy families, attended services and events and helped maintain the property. Yukiko's first friends were the wives of the Japanese clergy. After one of Yukiko's younger sisters, Masuko, arrived in America to marry Charles's friend, Henry Kiyomi Akiyama, there are photos of them together on the Cole Ranch and the Furuta farm. Life in America was becoming more familiar.

As the Japanese community in coastal Orange County grew, there were more social events that brought people together, such as *Oshogatsu* (New

Charles M. Furuta displaying his ambidextrous tennis swing. *Furuta family collection.*

Year's), the annual Japanese Association picnic in a downtown Huntington Beach park, the July 4 events in Huntington Beach and outings to the beach. Yukiko remembered cooking Sunday dinners with other families at the farm, the noise of children running in and out and playing traditional games such as *go* (a board game with stones) or *karuta* (a poetry card game).

The Furutas had six children: Raymond, Toshiko, Nobuko, Kazuko, Etsuko and Grace Emiko. Most were born at home at the Cole Ranch, but Grace Emiko was born at a hospital. Etsuko was born on the Furuta farm. The family was attended to by Dr. Jesse Burlew from Santa Ana (one of the pioneer doctors of St. Joseph Hospital in Orange County). These were the days when doctors made house calls. Yukiko thought that "maybe he charged more money if the family was more affluent. If he knew that a family was very poor, he didn't charge much. He was a respectful, kind, and nice doctor."

The Furuta family owned the farm for almost a century, first creating a goldfish farm and, later, a flower farm. Charles added on to the bungalow and barn as the family grew, when indoor plumbing arrived in Wintersburg and as crops changed.

As the farm developed, sheep periodically were rented from other farmers—joined by what one early Wintersburg resident described as a "massive rabbit"—to wander between the ponds to keep down weeds. Free-ranging chickens provided fresh eggs; decades later, one particular chicken,

George, is remembered by the family. Blackberry brambles grew near the barn, and violet wisteria blossoms cascaded from a nearby arbor. Pepper tree berries near the mission turned deep red in the summer. Residents of the manse remember the fragrance of the flower crops, sweet peas and water lilies creating a "special world."

The open land on the north side of the Furuta farm and the Wintersburg Mission—fronting the once muddy country lane that grew to become Wintersburg Avenue—was encroached upon with the widening of the street as the community grew. More homes and businesses dotted the countryside.

POSTON

The shock and disruption of World War II evacuation and incarceration marked another turning point for the Furutas, as it did for all Japanese families on the West Coast. Charles's four-decade effort to put down roots and support the community's development was turned against him during that time. His position as president of the Smeltzer Japanese Association and as one of the few landowners put the Wintersburg goldfish farmer under suspicion.

Charles first was taken to Tuna Canyon, an immigration detention center at Tajunga, Los Angeles County. Next, he was taken to the Lordsburg, New Mexico military detention center, along with other community leaders, clergy and teachers. Charles Furuta was sixty-one years old and had lived in America more than two-thirds of his life.

Learning they would go to the Colorado River Relocation Center at Poston, Arizona, Yukiko and her children packed, sealing precious items in boxes for storage at a house owned by brother-in-law Henry Akiyama. Two Huntington Beach families—Lopp and DaLaverne, whose daughters were good friends with the Furuta girls—are remembered by Yukiko, making them lunch before they left and the DaLaverne family accompanying them to the bus that would take them to Arizona.

Arriving at Poston, Yukiko found the rough wood barracks only had mattresses and no other furniture. With Charles incarcerated in another state, Henry Akiyama, then fifty-six, pulled boards from a pile of lumber left in the camp and made a long table and benches for his sister-in-law, a place for the family to sit together. Wind and dust blew through the barrack walls, as the green lumber dried out in the desert sun, leaving gaps. Yukiko recalls washing the floor so often she was left with a deformed finger she called her "memorial" of Poston.

The map for Poston's Block 12, Camp 1, includes the Furutas—Charles, Yukiko and their daughters, ranging from sixteen to twenty-seven—living next to their twenty-nine-year-old son, Raymond; his wife, Martha; and their newborn, Kenneth. On the other side of Raymond and Martha were Henry and Masuko Akiyama and their twenty-year-old son, Joe. Within the small barrack apartments, families strung up curtains to create rooms and privacy.

On the other side of Block 12 lived Reverend Sohei Kowta—the Furutas' Wintersburg neighbor and Wintersburg Japanese Presbyterian Church clergyman—with his wife, Riyo, and their children: Tadashi, Makoto and Hiroko, then thirteen, eleven and nine years old.

In Camp 3, lived another of the Wintersburg Japanese Presbyterian Church's clergymen, Reverend Kenji Kikuchi and his family. Kikuchi had been instrumental in building the new church during the Great Depression and had stayed ten years in Wintersburg, the longest tenure of all the clergymen at the church.

The barracks provided no place to cook for family meals; everyone was required to eat at a communal mess hall at the end of the camp. Laundry was done in a large communal room. Mail was inspected and censored. Families normally connected were sometimes fractured by the experience.

Eventually, most of the Furuta daughters were allowed to leave the camp for Minneapolis. Toshiko had a job with an oil company before evacuation and was able to arrange a transfer to Texas by living with a Caucasian family she had known in Huntington Beach. She later voluntarily returned to Poston to help look after her mother.

During that time, Toshiko worked to persuade the U.S. government to allow her father, Charles, to leave the Lordsburg, New Mexico detention center where he had been confined separately from his family. She was successful, and Charles was reunited with his family at Poston.

Etsuko also stayed at Poston to be with her new husband, Dan Fukushima (the future president of the United States High School Basketball Coaches Association), who she had married in the camp.

THE POETRY OF EARTH

Three years passed at Poston before Charles and Yukiko were allowed to leave. Yukiko left before Charles, riding in the back of an empty milk delivery truck, returning to Orange County with Henry Akiyama and a couple who worked at his goldfish farm. Arriving in Wintersburg, she found the house "in bad condition" and the goldfish ponds and land taken over by thick brush.

"She couldn't tell where the fish ponds were," explained her interpreter in 1982. "It took them almost two and a half years to clean up all the mess. She heard from other people that the people who rented this house caught fish and sold them. The ponds were all dried up, and there was no fish there."

Yukiko spent days cleaning the house, and—after Charles returned home—they began the long process of recovering the farm. After years in the barren desolation of the Arizona desert, Yukiko "remembered when they grew sweet peas before the war that the plants grew very well" and that her neighbor Riyo, Reverend Kowta's wife, "always admired the sweet peas."

Finding water lily roots were still alive under the weeds and muck, they began to cultivate lilies in the former goldfish ponds. The Furutas would

Etsuko, Kazuko, Nobuko, Toshiko and Raymond Furuta on Sunday, January 10, 1926, at the south side of the Furuta home. *Furuta family collection.*

become the only known providers of cut water lilies to florists in the United States during the last half of the twentieth century.

Looking back, Yukiko recalled it "took so long to change the pond into a field. That was very hard work." As time passed, "they became happy in the sweet pea business."

The Furuta farm in Wintersburg Village—owned by a Japanese family during a time when Japanese weren't legally allowed to own property or become citizens—had survived earthquakes, floods and the traumatic upheaval of World War II. Their land in Wintersburg, once again, became home.

Chapter 3

WELCOME TO THE PEATLANDS

Farmers, Preachers, Tycoons, Oil Men and Outlaws

W intersburg was not a completely sleepy little village of farms and churches. It was, after all, a frontier. The latter part of the nineteenth century and early part of the twentieth century saw the convergence of a truly unique assortment of people, destined to shape Southern California into a place unlike any other.

Described as a land filled with tules and referred to as the willows or peatlands, the Wintersburg area had been home to the Tongva (also referred

The Grand Army of the Republic encampment at the annual gathering of Civil War veterans at Huntington Beach, California, circa 1900. *City of Huntington Beach archives.*

to as the Kizh, or Gabrieleño) for at least nine thousand years. The peatlands and sea provided everything that was needed: game, shellfish and warm sunny days.

FARMERS AND RANCHERS

By the mid-1800s, more white settlers were moving in to buy land from the Spanish ranchos. The Tongva were still present, with campsites "in the Newport Beach area and on the Costa Mesa bluffs, and in the Wintersburg District," notes a publication of pioneer memories captured in 1983.

"They used to skirt the more populated town and ride their ponies to [the] back door," a descendant of Jacob R. Ross, one of Orange County's early pioneer families, says of the native Californians who visited her grandmother to share in the coffee and freshly baked biscuits.

"They never came empty handed," she recalls of the Tongva. "Sometimes they would bring a young rabbit or a few quail and sometimes a wild duck."

The county provided plenty of food. There are descriptions of wild grapes hanging in the oak and sycamore trees, which settlers used to make wine and vinegar. Blackberries grew along the riverbed. There was wild game, ducks and geese. Cattles and wild horses roamed the land, as ranchland gave way to farmland.

Japanese farmers on horseback at Irvine, Orange County, circa 1920. *California State University Fullerton, Center for Oral and Public History PJA 497.*

The early farmers plowed the earth around their campsites to clear brush for fear of fire and due to the rattlesnakes that lived in the tules. They worked continually to keep the coyotes and wild pigs from eating their chickens and the rabbits from eating their crops.

Horse Thieves

The ranchos made money from the sale of their land; however, not all Spanish and Mexican ranchers were happy to see the new pioneers, who often turned out their cattle to graze on farming land. The *Pioneer Memories* of the Ross family notes that "there was a herd law of sorts, but they paid little attention to it. There were no fences, and boundaries were marked by cattle bones or large boulders."

Farmers kept loaded shotguns to scatter loose cattle, mustangs and ranchers who trampled crops. And horse thieving was a problem. The settlers had brought with them the larger eastern-bred horses that were prized over the smaller local mustangs.

There was an unspoken law of hospitality—riders were allowed to switch mounts at ranches, picking a horse marked with the brand of a ranch in the direction they were headed. But, as the Ross pioneer memories explain, if the rider "left an unbranded horse, or one that was known to be stolen, the farmers got together and formed a posse and went after the man. They thoroughly enjoyed this break from their hard farm work."

The Ross family kept their horses "under lock and key so that they would have a mount when they had to go after horse thieves." In one incident, the settlers discovered that an enterprising local, Juan Diaz, was actually running a horse thieving ring and collecting rewards for returning horses he had stolen.

They brought Diaz back to the livery in Santa Ana and—in true western justice style—"hung him by the rafters until he confessed." Diaz told them he had a partner who hid the horses on his ranch in Santa Ana Canyon until the rewards for their return were offered. Reprieved from hanging, Diaz spent three years thinking about his crimes in San Quentin.

HIDDEN IN THE TULES

Farmers also found they had to deal with more than cattle and horse thieves on their land. The December 18, 1894 *Los Angeles Herald Examiner* reported that one Wintersburg farmer's plow unearthed a skeleton.

"From what can be learned it is probable that the discovery will lead to the unearthing of a murder of years ago," reported the *Examiner*. "The skeleton is in fair state of preservation, and is that of a comparatively young man. One man who claims to have seen it states...that the bones belonged to a man that was murdered. A few years ago, several people who had located on the ranch disappeared and no trace of them was ever found."

The *Examiner*—in typical journalistic fashion of its time—concluded the article by stating, "The list of these persons cannot be found tonight." (And the list was not found by the next morning, either.)

OILMEN (AND OUTLAWS)

It was about this time that there are local reports about oilman Gray Garrett Southern. Southern lived on the outskirts of Wintersburg near the Buck Ranch, located in the vicinity of Edwards Street and Varsity Drive in present-day Huntington Beach.

The April 9, 1896 *San Francisco Call* reported Southern was found guilty for the murder of Mariano Cuero in the midst of a "drunken brawl" in 1894. The *Call* previously reported in January 1896 that Southern had been charged, held without bail and taken by Sherriff Nichols to Los Angeles for safekeeping.

Southern was sentenced to serve twelve years in the penitentiary but managed to get a new trial after seven months, and the case was dismissed. By November 1908, he was back in trouble with the law. The *Los Angeles Herald Examiner* reported Southern was charged with "shooting at Constable Langto of Wintersburg, with intent to kill." Southern's wife, Nancy, reported that he "fired at her with a revolver and chased her to the house of a neighbor, half a mile distant." Sherman Buck and his sister-in-law Mrs. Charles Buck responded to the call for help.

The *Examiner* continued:

> *When Constable Langto and his party arrived at Southern's home* [he]
> *came out of the house armed with a shotgun and revolver...charging*

Langto and Buck with interfering in his private affairs, [he] *threatened to shoot Buck. Langto attempted to pacify Southern, when the latter suddenly turned the gun in Langto's direction and fired at him point blank, the charge passing so close to Langto's head as partially to deafen him. Buck sprang upon Southern, and, with Langto's assistance, Southern was overpowered, disarmed and taken to jail.*

The *Examiner* also reported that Southern's wife, Nancy, filed for divorce after the attempted murder. They apparently worked things out. A 1920s Orange County directory lists them together again with an address on Wintersburg Road.

TYCOONS, BARONS AND GUN CLUBS

As if this sort of behavior wasn't enough for farmers to contend with, in came the railroad tycoons, land barons and wealthy duck hunters.

Local landowners—in what was then known as Pacific City—convinced Henry Huntington to bring his Pacific Electric Railway into town, promptly renaming it Huntington Beach. The railway track ran along the beach, stopping in front of the wooden pier near Main Street and Ocean Avenue, in the area of the present-day pier off Pacific Coast Highway.

With the train came land speculators and real estate enterprises. However, Wintersburg was still considered "in the country," and going "to town" in Huntington Beach was an event.

Gun clubs began to sprout up in the wetlands areas of the peatlands, attracting some of Southern California's wealthiest businessmen and assorted celebrities and royals. One of the wealthiest hunting lodges was located near the outskirts of Wintersburg: the Bolsa Chica Gun Club

The October 15, 1905 *Los Angeles Herald* reported the opening of hunting season: "There was an exodus of khaki-clad men from Los Angeles last night. Trolley cars and trains took them away by hundreds, and automobiles and livery rigs conveyed scores to the chaparral and the club houses by the shores."

"Down at the club houses last night," continued the *Herald*, "there were merry crowds of sportsmen who burned good tobacco and drew the long bow until the momentous hour when the dice were rolled for the first choice of blind and first gun."

During the start of the 1908 hunting season, the *Los Angeles Herald* reported, "On most of the preserves the club houses and lodges are comfortably—some even luxuriantly—arranged with kitchens, snug sleeping quarters and elegant dining rooms." The previous year, the *Herald* had noted that "quantities of food supplies have been laid in, to say nothing of liquid refreshments, the latter to prevent members of taking cold when they get wet. Needless to say, all hunters will be very cautious not to fall into the water or get their feet wet." The hunters employed young boys to wade into the water and flush out ducks for their sport.

Memberships in the Bolsa Chica Gun Club initially started at $1,000 and later rose to $75,000, making the club more exclusive. Some members of the 3,400-acre club were staggeringly wealthy for the time and were valued for their sporty quality or that they were conveniently well connected.

The following is a sample of the club's members:

Austrian Count Jaro von Schmidt

A count in pre–World War I Germany, Schmidt was the owner and founder of the Bolsa Chica Gun Club. He owned a Tudor-style estate in Chester Place, Los Angeles, an early millionaire-row neighborhood. The count also owned a home in Tustin in Orange County and befriended Polish actress Madame Helena Modjeska, who had established a home in Santiago Canyon. Von Schmidt was known in Los Angeles social circles for his short stories and musical compositions. A philanthropist, art collector and self-described capitalist, von Schmidt was an avid hunter. He faced some criticism for his sport when he was reportedly "killing big bags of doves" in the countryside of Los Angeles County. Orange County lore has Count von Schmidt paying young boys to kill hummingbirds, which he then preserved for Victorian-style display or ladies' hats.

Hulett C. Merritt

Merritt was described by the December 11, 1910 *Los Angeles Herald* as a "millionaire and financier" in an article about the planned Merritt Building in downtown Los Angeles. At the time, Merritt was pushing city leaders to waive building height restrictions from 180 feet to 233 feet. Merritt is reported as saying he would scrap plans for the Italian Renaissance–style monument to his family unless he was allowed the height variance, otherwise "its beauty will be marred and I want to build for the artistic value more than for any profit I may get out of it." Originally from Minnesota, Merritt had sold his interests in the Merritt-Rockefeller syndicate in 1891 for more than $81 million.

William Bayly

A colleague of H.E. Huntington, Bayly helped develop the West Coast's version of Naples. The Baylys' European travels, soirees and "delightfully appointed" luncheons at 10 Chester Place—just a few doors down from Count von Schmidt's house at Chester Place—were regular features of the Los Angeles society pages.

Dr. G. MacGowan

A Los Angeles physician, Dr. MacGowan was once attacked by a Mrs. Robertson with a horsewhip. As reported in the April 18, 1896 *San Francisco Call*, "The doctor today received a note from the woman…'I warn you not to say anything further about the insanity theory' intimating there would be more horse-whipping if he attempted to prove her insane."

Jared Sidney Torrance

A multimillionaire Pasadena resident, Torrance was the director of the Pacific Steel Company. With others, he purchased part of the Rancho San Pedro land and—hiring well-known landscape architect Frederick von Olmstead and architect Irving Gill—went about creating a planned community, eventually named the City of Torrance. Brokering deals for Home Telephone Company, Torrance was questioned by the San Francisco grand jury in 1907 for a fund of $300,000 "for use in bribing the supervisors to grant the Home Company the competitive franchise." In *California in Our Time*, Robert Glass Cleland writes, "Under the state's promise of immunity, eighteen of the supervisors confessed the wholesale acceptance of bribes, not only from the organized activities of the underworld but on a still larger scale from public utilities and other corporations doing business in the city."

Isaac Milbank

Milbank was a member of the Dominguez Field aviation committee, a director of the Sinaloa Land Corporation and a director of the Pacific Mutual Life Insurance Company. In 1910, Milbank was involved with an infamous aerial duck hunt over Bolsa Chica by French aviator Hubert Latham and was present four days later when American aviator Arch Hoxsey broke the world record for altitude in a Wright biplane, flying 11,474 feet. He also witnessed the overly dramatic Latham crash his monoplane at a windy Dominguez Field the same day and set the remains on fire.

ONE HUNDRED DAM YEARS

The Bolsa Chica Gun Club started a royal battle when it dammed up the tidal flow into the wetlands to create more duck habitat, flooding farmland and obstructing waterways.

A 1910 *Forest and Stream* describe the 3,400-acre Bolsa Chica Gun Club as sixty miles of channels that became "barren salt marsh" at low tide. The gun club constructed a dam and four cement spillways with automatic gates to control the water's depth in the wetlands. It then developed thirty artesian wells with freshwater overflow "from several hundred more (wells) in the drainage district," ultimately changing the wetlands from a saltwater to freshwater marsh. The gun club then added nonnative plants and spread cow manure around the wetlands to develop earthworm and insect habitat. Its efforts to attract more game birds worked; however, local ranchers and farmers were cut off from three miles of ocean inlets.

There are news reports of farmers sabotaging dredging equipment and filing legal complaints, citing the dams were a violation of maritime law. In 1903, the War Department refused the Farmers Club's request to order the dam removed as an obstruction of navigable waters. Undeterred, a reported four-hundred farmers and ranchers forwarded a petition in 1905 to President Franklin Roosevelt, asking him to enforce maritime law and have the dam removed. In August 1907—after years of fighting and legal actions—the Bolsa Chica Gun Club offered a $500 reward "for the arrest of the persons who scuttled its dredger in Fremont Creek last week."

The farmers repeatedly lost this battle to the more moneyed and powerful tycoons of the twentieth century, but the tidal water turned in the twenty-first

French aviator Hubert Latham, circa 1910, around the time of his infamous airborne duck hunt over the Bolsa Chica wetlands. *George Bantham Baine Collection, Library of Congress, LC-USZ62-108159.*

century. One hundred years after the inlets were dammed by the gun club, the tidal flow of the Pacific Ocean into the Bolsa Chica Wetlands reopened on the dawn of August 24, 2006, cheered by a gathering of locals. Efforts to reestablish the wetland's natural habitat continue today.

LOS ANGELES HERALD: FRIDAY MORNING, DECEMBER 23, 1910.

AVIATOR DEFEATS BIRDS IN A RACE

Just Going for Little Spin. Says Latham at Start of Remarkable Flight

NO ACCIDENTS TO MAR FEAT

Novel Hunt Preceeded by a Fast Trip to Grounds of Bolsa Chica Gun Club

Snapshot of Hubert Latham and His Antoinette in Pursuit of Ducks Above the Surf Near Bolsa Chica

PARMELEE COMES HERE WITH HIS BABY WRIGHT

Ohio Man's Little Craft. Said to Be Speed Marvel. Is Entered in Meet

BEACHEY AND RADLEY FLY IN TRYOUTS FOR MEET

Newcomer to the Curtiss Forces Passes Most of Afternoon in the Air

CITY HALL'S PINE GUARD FELLED ON ANNEX SITE

DEAL FOR NEW MOTION PICTURE THEATER CLOSED

New Show House to Be Erected in South Main Street

COUNCILMEN WILL PROBE ACCOUNTS OF CITY CLERK

Public Welcome to Watch Work of Committee

LOS ANGELES BELIEVED TO HAVE WON RATE CASE

HOSPITAL IS READY TO RECEIVE INJURED AIRMEN

Hubert Latham's infamous duck hunt by plane over the Bolsa Chica on December 23, 1910, *Los Angeles Herald. Chronicling America, Library of Congress.*

Even a century earlier, the gun clubs periodically found out they were not above the law. In a reckless display of bravado, wealthy French aviator Hubert Latham flew his plane over the Bolsa Chica Gun Club, shooting ducks while in flight. He flew twenty-four miles to and from Dominguez Field in Los Angeles County to perform the feat for moneyed club members and media, who expressed amazement he had flown for half an hour "far out over the ocean."

Latham was the first person to have attempted a crossing of the English Channel in an airplane. His attempt was unsuccessful, and—although not part of his original plan—he inadvertently became the first person to land a plane on water.

The December 23, 1910 *Los Angeles Herald Examiner* reported that "the first duck brought down by [Latham] was brought to Los Angeles by Count von Schmidt and will be stuffed and presented to Latham as a trophy for making the first aviation hunt on record." Latham is reported to have commented afterward that he's "had a fine hunt, thank you. I think next time I'll be able to do much better." Latham added that his Antoinette airplane traveled faster than the ducks "so, in a flight of any length, I would have no trouble in overtaking them, for they tire and the machine does not." Landing a short distance from the Bolsa Chica Gun Club, Latham was met by a club member and invited for breakfast.

Two days later, the *San Francisco Call* reported Latham's stunt would make California "the first state in the union and the first government in the world to prohibit the hunting of wild game from air ships if the state fish and game commission has its way." The commission stated Latham frightened "thousands of ducks and geese so badly that they have not yet returned to the marsh."

The Fish and Game Commission further stated it feared others would try to copy Latham, stating "within the year it might become the fashion to hunt ducks and geese in aeroplanes over all the state." Awkwardly, M.J. Connell, reported by the *Los Angeles Herald Examiner* to be the president of the commission, was also a member of the Bolsa Chica Gun Club.

Hubert Latham in Antoinette, circa 1911, possibly at the Dominguez Airfield in Los Angeles County. *Library of Congress, LC-USZ62-36410.*

PREACHERS

By 1902, Presbyterian and Methodist Evangelical preachers had entered the fray, spreading their message of faith and temperance to farmers and field hands in the peatlands. The preachers traveled by horseback and wagon, walking into the fields. A large Methodist auditorium was constructed in Huntington Beach, the land around it hosting annual tent cities for Methodists and other community gatherings. The residents in Wintersburg called a village meeting to talk about building churches.

By 1910—at the opening of the whitewashed, wooden Japanese Mission in Wintersburg—Reverend John Junzo Nakamura recalled the founding in 1904 and the "earnest desire for mission work for the Japanese in this locality among the zealous members of the Presbyterian and M.E. churches in Westminster, California."

Yukiko Furuta, holding a bouquet of wildflowers at her new home in Wintersburg Village, circa 1912–13. *California State University Fullerton, Center for Oral and Public History, PJA 312.*

The itinerant mission work by Reverend Nakamura and others included the growing villages of Wintersburg, Bolsa, Garden Grove, Old Newport and Talbert. Nakamura reported traveling 225 miles throughout Orange County to visit Japanese laborers and families on farms and in labor camps as part of his regular circuit. At that time, there were over three hundred Japanese immigrants living year-round in the county, increasing by at least four hundred more during seasonal crop work.

During the mission's first five years, Nakamura reported it converted "fifteen souls"—the first being Charles Mitsuji Furuta—and raised $1,500 to build the mission "by the aid of our countrymen and some good American friends." The interfaith effort was entirely self-supported, relying on local donations in the community. Caucasian Presbyterian clergy and community members from Westminster, Smeltzer and Wintersburg (Reverend H.C. Cockrum, Mr. H. Larter and Mr. C.C. Johnson) joined Japanese representatives as mission trustees, including two future goldfish farmers: Charles Furuta and Tsurumatsu Asari.

The Wintersburg Mission became tangible proof that despite a frequent Wild West atmosphere—and despite California's restrictions on Japanese immigrants—a Japanese community was gathering. The same tules that had served as an out-of-the-way place for tycoons and outlaws to stretch or break the law while hidden from public view became a "gospel swamp." The peatlands were on their way to becoming civilized.

Chapter 4

CELERY'S MAGICAL POWERS

In the early 1900s, the entire country seems to have been enamored of celery. Celery was the super food of the early twentieth century, and its promoters promised good health and weight loss. Early vegetarianism advocates were recommending recipes chockfull of celery. And in Wintersburg, farmers were toiling to meet the demand. Like Wintersburg's other famous crop, chili peppers, celery growing was backbreaking work. Chili peppers would eventually overtake celery as the dominant crop—after the celery blight—but in the first decade of 1900, the fields of Wintersburg had a distinct green peppery scent.

The September 1905 *Los Angeles Herald* published a charming student report on its front page written by Pearl Palla, age eleven years, entitled "How to Raise Celery": "In the peat lands celery can be grown in beds and by June the plants are ready to be set in fields. The plants are pulled, the tops trimmed to make the celery more bushy, then the roots are set in deep furrows. Boys and girls can help do this work."

Probably not an opinion shared by the men working long hours in the celery fields.

Miss Pearl continues:

> *Celery is carefully cultivated. As the plants grow, the dirt is gradually filled in the furrows. When about ready for market, the dirt is banked around the celery nearly to the top, where it is left for about two weeks to bleach. The stalks turn from dark green to a creamy white. Then the field is plowed and*

Japanese American workers on a celery farm at Huntington Beach, circa 1920. *California State University Fullerton, Center for Oral and Public History, PJA 286.*

the roots are cut with a celery cutter. Men trim and crate the stalks and then the celery is sent to market.

The peat lands have been low and swampy, but when they are drained and cultivated they are very rich. Here in California, they use peat shoes on the horses. The shoes are made of square boards that are fastened on horses' feet to keep them from sinking in the damp soil.

The white plume and golden heart varieties of celery are most generally raised. The golden heart is a self bleacher. A celery field is a beautiful sight, with its long, straight rows of green plants.

In November 1905, a year after the Pacific Electric Railway line traveled through the peatlands into Huntington Beach, *Los Angeles Herald* headlines shouted, "Peat Lands Now Worth Hundreds of Dollars an Acre." The *Herald* reported, "One of the most interesting sights in western wonderland is that of the celery trains which roll out of Smeltzer [present-day north Huntington Beach]." The Southern Pacific Railroad's branch line stopped near Smeltzer Avenue and Wintersburg Avenue—now Edinger and Warner Avenues—to load produce. The turn-of-the-century tracks remain there today, fading into the dirt.

"Seventeen carloads [of] celery are now sent forward, bound for the large cities of the east," continued the *Herald.* "Three thousand seven hundred

Horse with peat shoes. *San Francisco Call* from June 8, 1902. *Chronicling America, Library of Congress.*

and fifty dollars are the figures at which these daily shipments are valued and so heavy is the demand for the Thanksgiving trade that there is much doubt as to all of the orders being filled."

Cutting celery in Huntington Beach, 1913. *California State University Fullerton, Center for Oral and Public History, PJA 286.*

The *Herald* extolled the peatlands, albeit with a bit of a backhanded compliment: "When one considers that it was by chance this great industry was started, the contrast of ten years ago from today, is amazing. Before that time the peatland section of Orange county was considered both useless and dangerous and was inhabited by a low class of Americans who earned a livelihood by selling the peat cut from their lands."

"The peatland, formerly worth less than $5 an acre, now readily brings $200 and often rents for $40 an acre for the one crop," reported the *Herald*, noting that three thousand acres were planted in celery—making the Orange County celery fields one of the largest in the world—and that "undoubtedly the production will be much larger in 1906."

By 1905, farmers had formed the Celery Growers' Association, which organized final cultivation, blanching and field irrigation, as well as "cutting, tieing, crating and carloading." Growers netted about fifteen cents for each dozen of celery plants, which the *Herald* reported was a "handsome profit" since the cost of production was fifty to sixty dollars an acre.

In 1907, a reported 144 Japanese farms and over 5,100 acres were in production. By 1909—a year after celery blight hit Orange County—the Smeltzer, Wintersburg and Talbert farmers had lost some but still had 5,000 acres in production. Masakazu Iwata notes in his extensive study, *Planted in Good Soil*, that "each season, from Thanksgiving to March of the following year, Smeltzer celery monopolized the American celery market."

Celery wasn't just for Thanksgiving. An entire industry of fresh market celery, tonics, sodas and elixirs had swept the country. Paine's Celery

Second Section

LOS ANGELES HERALD

City News

WEDNESDAY MORNING, NOVEMBER 22, 1905.

CELERY SHIPPING IS IN FULL SWAY

ENTIRE TRAINLOAD SENT OUT DAILY

CELERY GROWING IS GREAT INDUSTRY AT SMELTZER

A Field of Celery

An Artesian Well by Which Celery Lands Are Watered

ASK IMMEDIATE INCORPORATION

RAILWAYS MAKE MOVE IN WILMINGTON CASE

QUESTIONS POWER OF POLICE BOARD

MAY HAVE NO RIGHT TO REFUSE LICENSES

SUGGESTS REFORMS IN METHOD OF TAXATION

STATE TAX COMMISSION ISSUES STATEMENT

Only 27 More Shopping Days Until Christmas

Toyland and Dolldom

"The Ebell" Shoe for Women

Hamburger's Millinery Inimitable

—In Style, Quality and Price—

$15.00 Dress and Suit Hats

The Only Gloves That Save You Money in Buying

Women's $1.50 Real Kid Gloves

$1.05

Hosiery and Knit Underwear

Women's 80c Allover Lace Lisle Hose   29c

Ruffs, Neckwear Ribbons

$7.50 Silk Ruffs, Capes and Scarfs, choice $3.98

Celery growing is a great industry at Smeltzer. *Los Angeles Herald*, November 22, 1905. *Chronicling America, Library of Congress.*

Compound advertisements—found in every major newspaper—touted celery's ability to cleanse blood, cure nerves and act as a cure-all for tired women and infirm children that has "made people well when every other

Paines Celery Compound ad in the *Scranton Tribune* from February 20, 1901. It was next to an article about a newfangled solar motor experiment in Southern California. *Chronicling America, Library of Congress.*

remedy has failed." Dr. Brown's Celery Tonic (still sold as Dr. Brown's Cel-Ray soda) was a popular item in New York delicatessens, viewed as a quasi-medicinal drink.

In the twenty-first century, the magical powers of celery are back in the news. Men's health magazines now advise that eating celery releases the steroid androstenone, creating pheromones that attract women, concluding that the centuries-old beliefs about its aphrodisiac qualities may be true. Much like the advertisements of one hundred years ago, celery colognes, juices and tonics again are making promises to an eager public.

Chapter 5

COLE RANCH AND THE

UNIVERSE EFFIGY

W intersburg, it seems, has always been a place where people gather, share their lives and practice their faith. In addition to the mission and churches that date back to the early 1900s, there is evidence of spiritual practices dating back thousands of years, when Wintersburg was the land of the Tongva or Kizh.

Friar Geronimo Boscana writes his observations of the life and practices of the first Southern Californians in *Chinigchinich* in 1846. It is a decidedly ethnocentric view—Boscana was not an objective party—but a few insights can be gleaned.

Boscana reports the belief that when the body died, the heart remained "to dwell among the stars, and like them throw its light upon the earth. For

Cole Ranch in Wintersburg. *Furuta family collection.*

Raymond and Toshiko Furuta at the Cole Ranch, 1916. *Furuta family collection.*

this reason, they said that the planets, and most luminous bodies, were their hearts, or in other words, they were themselves, in reality."

When the Tongva looked into the night sky, they saw themselves. They were part of the universe.

WINTERSBURG'S COLE FAMILY

In 1898, the Cole family moved to California, eventually buying land in Wintersburg. Pioneer historian Samuel Armor writes that Myrtle Cecillian Cole was a New York lawyer who "took up agriculture and horticulture, farming twenty acres at Wintersburg...improved this place and afterward sold it, and then purchased the sixty-acre Ross ranch near Wintersburg." The Ross family recalled native Californian campsites in the "Wintersburg District."

Of M.C. Cole's four children, it is later noted in oral histories that his son, Homer, eventually joined his father in working the former Ross farm, continuing after M.C. Cole's death in 1916.

Sometime between 1902 and 1910, Homer Cole brought home to his wife, Jesse Hoffman Cole, a stone object found by a plowman working on the Cole Ranch. It was a perfect circle of chlorite schist with an indent and notches incised in what looks like a butterfly pattern at the top. To the Coles, it was probably an interesting curiosity.

To the Tongva, it was the universe.

REVISITING THE UNIVERSE EFFIGY

The Universe Effigy quietly resided at the Cole Ranch for over twenty-five years before being loaned to the Bowers Museum in 1936, catalog number 2878. Scholars recently took another look at it.

In their 2009 paper for the *Pacific Coast Archaeological Society Quarterly* (PCAS), Henry Koerper and Paul Chace write, "the Universe Effigy is arguably the most esthetically spectacular of all California magico-religious artifacts" and that the Cole Ranch discovery was "the first Universe Effigy to come to modern attention."

Other "universe effigies" have turned up along the Southern California coast, in San Mateo Canyon and in Riverside County. Koerper and Chace note that "nearly all of the effigies were fashioned from chlorite schist, perhaps mined on Catalina Island."

Koerper and Chace believe that there is a correlation between the effigies and ground paintings that conceptualize the universe and that the effigies were Chinigchinich objects used for female rites of passage. The universe representations include concentric rings indicating the Milky Way and the human spirit. Another scholarly view noted by Koerper and Chace posits the effigies may represent the "oval sacred enclosure, the wamkish, a ritual place for, among other things, initiations and ground paintings. The wamkish...stood as a microcosm of the earth and universe."

At some point, the lives of Wintersburg's first residents—the Tongva—and its later pioneers connected.

Masuko Yajima Akiyama and Yukiko Yajima Furuta at the Cole Ranch, 1915. *Furuta family collection.*

Before 1910, Wintersburg Japanese Presbyterian Mission congregants Charles Mitsuji Furuta and Henry Kiyomi Akiyama lived at the Cole family house on Gothard Street and worked on the ranch with M.C. and Homer Cole where the Universe Effigy was found. Furuta—known to be a fine horseman—worked the horses and Akiyama worked the land. Whether either found the effigy, or knew of it, is unknown.

Koerper and Chase refer to the effigy as a "portable cosmos" whose "morphology and design elements suggest a rich complexity of symbolic communications."

Scholar Charles Irwin, in a paper titled "A Material Representation of a Sacred Tradition," writes about the Universe Effigy that "every human society has a world view that includes the structure of the universe and earth, the origin and history of the society and its aspirations…our species has expressed sacred concepts in material symbolizations for millennia."

In simpler terms, the Universe Effigy is a reminder that nine thousand years ago, the Tongva saw more to life in Wintersburg—the sky above it and the earth beneath it—than what occupies it today.

Chapter 6

THE PLUNDER OF
BUCK RANCH

During the season of flowers, the females and children decked themselves in splendor; not only entwining them in the hair, but stringing them with the stalks and leaves, making boas of them.
The Indians of Los Angeles County: Hugo Reid's Letters of 1852

What lies beneath Wintersburg? More than the eye can see and much that has been lost.

It was December 1930. Workers on Wintersburg's old Buck Ranch—then being referred to as the Callens Ranch—found over a dozen skeletons and several large stone bowls. The Orange County Sheriff was called and sent deputies to inspect the site the next day. Their conclusion: it was a Native American burial ground. Someone contacted local collector Frederick R. Aldrich and, later, collector Herman Strandt, who is reported as supervising the remainder of the dig.

The *Huntington Beach News* reported on January 1, 1931, that "N. Acevedo, intelligent Spanish employee of the ranch and W. Peters, American employed on the ranch, plowing three feet deep in the field discovered the burial mound, Friday, December 26, when their plowshare turned out a skull." The men grabbed shovels and found more skulls and human bones.

Within days, more than five hundred people descended on the site, carting away "skulls and other relics." At least one hundred skulls were found by farm and oil workers, as well as curiosity seekers, according to archaeologist

Paul Chace in "Locating the Buck Ranch Prehistoric Burial Ground." Thousands of years of human history were picked apart and carted away to private collections.

CONFUSION AND STEREOTYPES

In "The Case of the Missing Buck Ranch Mortuary Remains: A Mystery Partly Solved," archaeologist Henry C. Koerper explains that "the first announcement of the discoveries appeared in a *Santa Ana Register*, December 27, 1930 article that was repeated by the paper on Monday followed by a December 29 story giving more specifics."

"Much of the archaeological information was in error," notes Koerper, "such as the idea that some of the deceased had been buried standing up, that all were male, that the area had possibly been the site of a great battle, and that these Indians raised corn."

"On December 30, the *Huntington Beach News* published its story and touted the Indian cemetery as 'believed to be the oldest in the State of California' yet later gave the estimated age of the burial ground as only about 200

The Shosuke Nitta farm in the peatlands, present-day McFadden Avenue and Fairview Street, circa 1907. *California State University Fullerton, Center for Oral and Public History, PJA 444.*

years," continues Koerper. The *Santa Ana Register* published a photograph "showing an excavator holding a skull in front of human skeletal remains in situ."

The dig went on through January 1931, when the *Huntington Beach News* again reported on the finds. Koerper writes that the article stated "the cemetery contained women, children and men, but erroneously reported that these people had raised corn, potatoes and tobacco."

At the time of the discovery, the Callens brothers were working oil leases on the Buck Ranch. Joseph Callens later served on the first Fountain Valley city council in 1957 with Charles Ishii and James Kanno, both American-born *Nisei*. Kanno later became the first Japanese American mayor in the mainland United States. Charles's father, Kyutaro Ishii, and James's father, Shuji Kanno, both *Issei*, were also both elders with the Wintersburg Japanese Presbyterian Mission.

In the rural peatlands communities—Wintersburg Village, Talbert, Bolsa and Smeltzer—everybody knew everybody, and the Buck Ranch find was front-page news.

THE PORTABLE COSMOS

The writer found both oblong and pyriform polished stones, such as have hitherto been considered, and described, as "plummets, plumb-bobs, sinkers, and weights." An old Tobikhar said that such stones would require too much time and labor to be used only to cast into the sea. The Indians term them "medicine stones," and consider them as possessing medicinal properties.
The Indians of Los Angeles County: Hugo Reid's Letters of 1852

Besides human remains believed to be the Tongva ("people of the earth" or Kizh), finds at the site included cogged stones, jewelry, abalone, arrowheads and a "portable cosmos," a multi-holed steatite tablet. Carved of stone most likely mined on Tongva quarries on Santa Catalina Island, references to the multi-holed stone tablet in newspaper reports were the subject of mystery to archaeological researchers until they realized it was right in front of them.

"This object had been described in contemporary newspaper accounts covering the Wintersburg dig, as having a constellation of features so distinct that it could easily be identified if rediscovered," write Henry Koerper and Joe Cramer in "Additional Multi Holed Tablets from the Fred Aldrich Collection." "The artifact is a thin tablet possessing 70 drilled holes."

The January 1, 1931 edition of the *Huntington Beach News* reported in a front-page article, "Indian Burial Ground Is Unearthed on Buck Ranch," that "there was a stone found which was four by five inches with the edges slightly rounded, and 70 small holes in even rows on the stone, the holes being near a quarter of an inch in diameter. That stone was either used in some game or for some unknown purpose. People versed in Indian lore said they had never seen such a relic."

It is on display at the Bowers Museum in Santa Ana, California. Much like the remarkable Universe Effigy found on the Cole Ranch in Wintersburg, the archaeologists noted the Buck Ranch finds have been "hiding in plain sight."

Other multi-holed tablets have been found and are included in the Bowers Museum collections. And like the cogged stones found in Wintersburg and the Bolsa Chica Wetlands, there is a lot of guessing about the purpose of the multi-holed tablets.

In the case of the Universe Effigy—or the Keystone Cache of cogged stones found on the Bolsa Chica—it is thought that important ceremonial objects were stored away from dwellings and included in important burials. The Keystone Cache appears to have been buried, encased in a mud slurry, while the tablet was part of a burial site.

Henry Wetherbee Henshaw, affiliated with the Smithsonian Museum and U.S. Geological Survey, wrote *Perforated Stones from California* in 1887. Although not specifically describing the cogged stones or multi-holed tablets found in Wintersburg, he noted that one California native woman he interviewed said, "We used to bury them with our dead."

Researchers also believe one of the burials at the Buck Ranch site was for a shaman or spiritual leader, due to the ornamentation and burial remains. The remains of a meticulously crafted limpet shell necklace and red stone smoking pipe held at the Bowers Museum are believed to belong to the shaman.

"There was one article made of clay. It was possibly an Indian pipe, the clay had apparently not been burned," reported the *Huntington Beach News*. "There were Indian stone bowls, used for grinding meal and the pestles that the Indians used to crush their corn into meal. One bowl weighed forty pounds and one pestle weighted nine pounds."

The former Buck Ranch land is now a tract of homes, developed in the late twentieth century.

THE ALDRICH COLLECTION

Frederick Randolph Aldrich operated a private museum on Balboa Island in Newport Beach for many years. When he passed in 1953, his "shell collection" was first purchased and displayed at the Balboa Pavilion, and later, portions of it ended up at the Bower's Museum.

"One of Nation's Finest Shell Collections Opens to Public Each Sunday on Bay Island," a local news item circa 1950, reports Aldrich's real break came "when a rancher at work with a sub soiler near the Bolsa Chica Gun Club, north of Huntington Beach, unearthed an Indian bowl. He contacted Aldrich and further probing was undertaken. The exploration resulted in the richest Indian cemetery ever found in California, Aldrich says. It yielded human remains, and numerous household, hunting and ceremonial articles. Aldrich has the finest relics of this find on exhibit."

Writing about the Buck Ranch archaeological finds in 2009, Henry Koerper notes, "There are 25 adults and three sub adults in the Aldrich Collection that had almost certainly come from Buck Ranch." Moe Gronsky (the Gronsky family owned the Balboa Pavilion on Balboa Island, Newport Beach) told researchers that "an unspecified number of skulls"

Examples of basketry of the Mission Indians of Southern California, Edward S. Curtis, circa 1924. *Library of Congress LC-USZ62-98667.*

were held and not transferred to the Bowers Museum. It is unknown where they are today.

THERE'S MORE

Archaeological finds in the mesas, lowlands and wetlands of Wintersburg indicate thriving populations with complex beliefs.

A recent environmental impact review prepared by the City of Huntington Beach for a mixed-use project at Beach Boulevard and Warner (Wintersburg) Avenue reported that "the Native American Heritage Commission identified the presence of Native American cultural resources within the immediate area…and noted that the general area was considered sensitive for cultural resources…representatives from the *Gabrieleno Tongva* Nation [express] their concerns about the sensitivity of the…area for Native American resources and burial grounds."

The conclusion in the report was that the area is "considered to be sensitive for the presence of Native American cultural resources, including human remains."

During the 1970s, human burials were discovered on the east side of Edwards Street (CA-ORA-82). In a report prepared for the U.S. Army Corps of Engineers in 1989, it was noted that the "deep deposits at this site appear to reflect lengthy use." A multiple burial site was found in the 1970s, 1,320 feet northwest of the Charles and Yukiko Furuta farm and Wintersburg Japanese Presbyterian Mission complex (Shell Midden, Site Number 30000346).

The effigy was found in the early 1900s just west of the Furuta farm off Wintersburg Avenue at the Cole Ranch. In the late 1860s, the Cole Ranch was owned by the Ross family who had reported that native Californians camped in the area.

On the Huntington Beach Mesa—where present-day Huntington Beach and Fountain Valley converge—there are discoveries of magico-religious items, charmstones, birdstones, cogged stones and pipes at the Dobkin site and sites along Beach Boulevard between Adams Avenue and Heil Avenue, as well as the Borchard Ranch, south of the old Buck Ranch, all in present-day Huntington Beach.

And there are the significant burial remains found at the Bolsa Chica Mesa and Bolsa Chica Wetlands. Over a dozen known archaeological cultural sites are scattered throughout the Bolsa Chica and Wintersburg lowlands alone, representing at least nine thousand years of occupation.

Oscar L. Stricklin, an oil worker who arrived in Huntington Beach in the 1920s, talked in 1971 with Costa Mesa's *Daily Pilot* newspaper about helping a farmer who had unearthed a mass grave near present-day Slater Avenue. Stricklin remembers this happening in the 1920s.

"Stricklin took some of his men to the grave and helped the farmer uncover 36 skeletons whose origin remain a mystery to him," reported *Daily Pilot*'s Rudi Niedzielski in "Oil Boom Recalled: Pioneer Writes of Huntington Era." Stricklin wrote about the incident in his memoirs several years before his passing in 1974.

"There were many in an area about 40 feet square. Some of them were actually sitting up, others were stooped over and some were lying down flat. We didn't take them out. We'd uncover them and get all the dirt away from them and just leave them sitting there. It was a gruesome sight," remembered Stricklin. "Nobody knows if it was a massacre or whether they had died and were put there or whether they drowned in a flood. We called the people from the state and they put them in a museum somewhere."

The continual drain of historic resources to unknown places is a century-old problem. With the constant discovery of new archaeological finds—combined with the concerns of the Tongva nation—it's reasonable to expect there will be more.

BACK TO BUCK RANCH

Of the hundreds of curious people who visited the burial spot of an unknown people, many carried away skulls and other relics.
Huntington Beach News, *January 1, 1931*

The *Huntington Beach News* account of the Buck Ranch discovery reports that "arrowheads, some quite large…were beautifully finished, the workmanship being quite smooth" and speculates that some were spearheads. "One skull found had fangs and was undoubtedly the head of a dog" continues the anonymous report. "The skulls and bodies bore evidence of having been laid out in graves."

The January 1, 1931 article considers the site could have been a mass grave from a battle or that "there may have been a marshy spring there and the Indians disposed of their dead in deposition of the bodies in the spring or march." This is refuted by present-day scholars. The *Huntington Beach News* then discusses the skulls, in ridiculous fashion.

"One skull brought out with the shovels had jaws hard set on two rows of teeth. The skull was smaller than the average found," writes the *Huntington Beach News*. "'That might be a woman's skull' suggested a digger. 'Impossible,' said his companion. 'No woman would ever keep her mouth shut that tight, or keep it shut that long.'"

It continues, "Another small skull was found with very low forehead. 'Possibly that may be a woman's skull,' was suggested," writes the *Huntington Beach News*. "'It was surely the skull of a very stupid human, but that is not a sure sign it is a woman's skull,' was the answer as the crowd of curious laughed."

Rarely has an article combined such serious scientific speculation with such inanely disrespectful commentary. Undoubtedly, this is the reason the article's author and those quoted wisely remained anonymous.

The *Huntington Beach News* ends the article: "The deputy sheriffs who visited the spot, carefully reinterred the bones they found unearthed, but others who followed after have dug the skeletons out again."

Chapter 7

THE WINTERSBURG MISSION

Why Orange County's Japanese Community Built a Church in Wintersburg Village

Faith spread the wings that crossed the sea,
To find this land for you and me;
And Faith did everything that we
Feel proud about.
Dr. Ernest Adolphus Sturge, 1903
Leader in the Japanese mission effort on the Pacific Coast

A century-old parchment held in the archive of the present-day Wintersburg Presbyterian Church—referred to by the church as "Reasons to Build a Church"—is much more than an early fundraising tool for the mission-building effort a century ago. It is a compelling document, placing the Wintersburg Mission in the context of the historic struggle for civil liberties and the desire to become American.

"In 1902 there arose an earnest desire for mission work for the Japanese in this locality among the zealous members of the Presbyterian and M.E. churches in Westminster, California," explains a church dedication program from 1934. Clergy members J.W. Miller and Joseph K. Inazawa, then an itinerant missionary, arrived in the spring of 1904 to look over the countryside of Orange County. Finding the area promising, they secured Episcopalian minister Hisakichi Terasawa—already an established clergy member and teacher in the San Francisco area. Terasawa formally established the mission effort in December 1904.

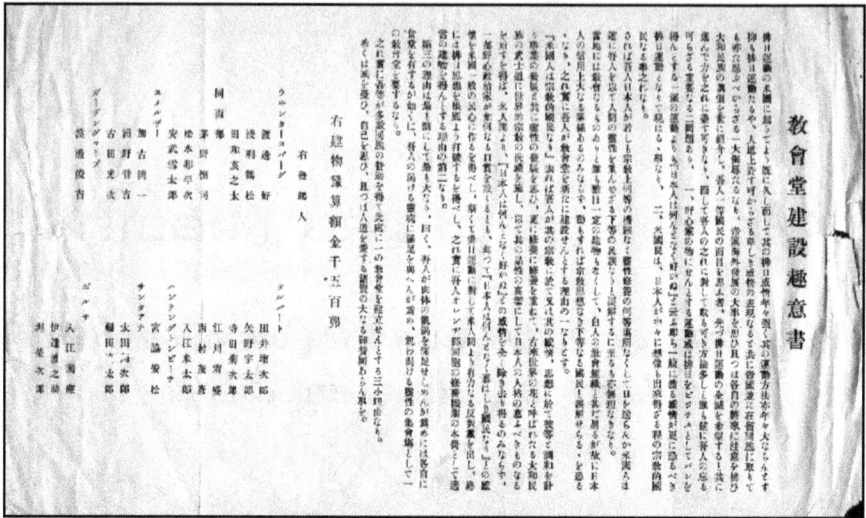

"Reasons to Build a Church" parchment used to fundraise for the Wintersburg Japanese Presbyterian Mission, circa 1904. *Wintersburg Presbyterian Church.*

The mission effort was at first supported by both the Presbyterian and Methodist churches as well as "good friends in the Westminster district," reports a church history. The group appealed to the Los Angeles Presbytery to help with the mission, but the Presbytery had no funds for the effort. The community then initiated a fundraising effort, receiving "substantial support" from the young people's society of the Christian Endeavor Union of Orange County.

Members of the Japanese community circulated the prospectus document throughout the countryside to explain their desire to build Orange County's first Japanese mission and their need for donations. The document acknowledges the anti-Asian sentiment of early 1900s California and the fact that European Americans did not understand them, their culture or their spirituality:

> *The growing intensity of the anti-Japanese movement which from an humanity's perspective should be impermissible is also a serious insult directed against the Japanese. From Japan's point of view, and that of the people who seek a future abroad, and those who want Japan to maintain its standing as a first rated nation, the complete elimination of an anti-Japanese movement is desired. Moreover, it is not just a matter of hoping that it will happen but working together to make it happen.*

In *California's Story*, a 1922 textbook "written to meet the State requirement for the teaching of the history of California," there is reference to the "Chinese question" and later the "Japanese question," both preceded by the "Indian question." Its authors write, "There has been a steady growth of trade with the great nations of the Orient, like China and Japan. The prosperity and good order of all these places is very directly of importance to California, for she has much trade with them."

California's Story continues:

> *In the case of Japan there has been trouble at times because of the coming of more Japanese to California than our people like to have living here and owning property in the state. But up to the present, in spite of outcries and angry talk on both sides, the wiser people of the state have tried to smooth out difficulties in a just way. In more ways than one, California and Japan need to be good friends, and this should be remembered whenever the "Japanese question" is talked about.*

Gathering together in a barn in Wintersburg—with the guidance and encouragement of clergy from nearby Westminster and Episcopalian minister Hisakichi Terasawa from San Francisco—representatives from the broader Orange County Japanese community attached their names to the document and initiated a plan of action:

> *Two important issues to consider to make this possible are: 1) There are people who are engaged in making the anti-Japanese movement a project, but the more worrisome issue is the growing feeling of people expressing a dislike of the Japanese even though there is no basis or particular reason for having this feeling; 2) Americans need to believe that the Japanese are religiously inclined, but if an organized endeavor or religious structure where their religion is practiced and developed is not visible, Americans will look down on the Japanese as a backward people who can live life without the necessity of a church where they can develop themselves.*

The Japanese recognized the symbolic nature of a church in American culture. Not only would it be a place for the Japanese immigrant community to gather and support each other, but it would also reassure European Americans that there was common ground, similar aspirations and a desire to become part of the community. A mission building, placed prominently in the open farmland of Wintersburg, would speak for the Japanese community.

Its members knew their Caucasian neighbors were unfamiliar with the rich history and culture of their homeland. The financial and social investment by the Japanese community represented by the construction of a mission would demonstrate that its members were equal to their neighbors:

> So even if we claim to have places of worship, without an actual structure (church), the Japanese, unlike Americans whose Caucasian social system is organized around a church, not having a church makes Americans distrustful of us and allows them to judge us a low class people to be looked down upon. That is the reason why we want to establish a church.

The pain of not being understood and the desire to assimilate into American culture permeates the document:

> One reason regarding point number two that makes building a church necessary is that Americans are very religious people, so if we can understand how they think and feel about religion, we can promote harmonious relations and work together. And if we can develop our own spirituality, then Americans will probably accept us, and we will be able to slowly incorporate their way of thinking into our bushido spirit, and by doing so it will show our worth and value to Americans, changing their attitude and eventually the anti-Japanese movement will disappear.

A significant cultural barrier was the lack of understanding by European Americans regarding the spiritual beliefs of the Japanese immigrants and of the concept of *bushido*. The use of the word is revealing in that many Japanese were emigrating because feudal samurai ways were ending. In several of the oral histories of Wintersburg, there is mention of a family having samurai roots.

Bushido, the Soul of Japan, penned by Inazo Nitobe in English in 1900, explains it is a "code of moral principles which the knights were required or instructed to observe," much like the code of chivalry understood in feudal Europe in which religion played a significant role. Orange County's Japanese residents knew *bushido* and Christianity were compatible:

> A second reason for building a church is that with a church and based on an understanding of Americans' religious point of view and incorporating their ideas into our bushido spirit, we can work diligently to train ourselves to be in harmony with American Christian ways. This will change their ideas

74

of why they dislike Japanese and they will find us attractive people. This is the reason why we Orange County comrades want a church.

A final reason for the church-building effort expressed in the document testifies to the simple need for a spiritual and community center: "It is a simple but a major third reason for building a church. Like people who are hungry who need a place that provides food, people who hunger for spiritual satisfaction need a place that provides it."

The parchment concludes with a call to action to the "many people who are concerned about Japan, or about our own situation, or what is right will participate in this endeavor." Setting a goal of $1,500, the "Reasons to Build a Church" document was signed by representatives of the Japanese community from around rural Orange County's small communities.

Names on the translated document include Yoshi Watanabe and Inota Tawa from Wintersburg (Huntington Beach); Tsuneji Kayano, Uheji Matsumoto and Yukitaro Yasutake from West Wintersburg (Huntington Beach); Seiichi or Kiyokazu Kako, Otokichi Urano and Mitsji or Mitsutsugu Koda from Smeltzer (Huntington Beach); Masujiro Tai, Utaro Yano, Kikujiro Terada, Hiromori Egawa, Shigehiko Nishimura and Kometaro Irie from Talbert (Fountain Valley); Shunkichi Watanabe from Garden Grove; Eijiro Hori, Kunizo Irie and Naminosuke Date from Bolsa (Westminster); and Naojiro Ota and Seitaro or Kiyotaro Fukuda from Santa Ana.

Also notable among the signatories was Tsurumatsu "T.M." Asari, one of Wintersburg's goldfish farmers, and Yasumatsu Miyawaki, reported to have owned the first Japanese grocery store in Huntington Beach in the Talbert-Leatherman Building (Huntington Beach's oldest wooden structure, 217 Main Street).

Yasumatsu Miyawaki, signator on mission prospectus, circa 1911. *California State University Fullerton, Center for Oral and Public History, PJA 030.*

The Rush to California

The early mission era in northwest Orange County was also the time of St. Louis, Missouri's Louisiana Purchase Exposition, a World's Fair at which California once again made a big impression on winter-fatigued easterners. The January 18, 1905 *Los Angeles Herald* reported on the impact California made, quoting Charles L. Wilson, California's superintendent of the installation of exhibits at the Louisiana Purchase Exposition: "Everywhere I heard people talking about California."

"When I left St. Louis, it was eight degrees below zero. It was fifteen below at Kansas City, and colder as we came through Kansas, with snow and sleet all the way to Needles, 300 miles east of Los Angeles," continued Wilson. Wilson's train arrived in San Bernardino at sunrise to clear, sunny skies. "People on the train who had never before gazed upon California scenery, and were a little doubtful of the truth of some of the glowing stories they had heard of the glorious southland, when they looked out of the car windows this morning were in ecstasies of delight."

The *Herald* also reported tourist travel to Southern California was growing, packing the Southern Pacific and Santa Fe railroads "to their fullest capacity. The larger hotels are rapidly filling up" and the Santa Fe "Pullman accommodations for lower berths on their limited out of Chicago have been exhausted."

Like those traveling by rail across country, California represented a new life for the Japanese. Many of the early arrivers were Buddhist, although many had already become acquainted with Christianity in Japan through the visits of American missionaries. Some of California's first ordained Japanese clergy were involved with the establishment of the mission building effort in Wintersburg.

The 1910 Mission

Reverend Junzo Nakamura arrived in 1909 to head the mission-building committee and oversee the construction of the mission and manse in Wintersburg Village. By May 8, 1910, the mission doors were officially opened at a ceremony joined by Reverend H.C. Cockrum of nearby Westminster and Dr. Ernest Adolphus Sturge, chair of the "Board of Foreign Missions," the Japanese mission effort for the Presbyterian Church on the West Coast.

IN COMMEMORATION

OF

The Sixth Anniversary of The Japanese Presbyterian Mission

OF

Wintersburg, Orange County, California

December 25, 1910

Program for the dedication of the Wintersburg Japanese Presbyterian Mission's first building—six years after the mission program was founded—featuring a photo of Reverend Junzo Nakamura. *Furuta family collection.*

Dr. Ernest Adolphus Sturge arriving at Yokohama, Japan, circa 1910–15. *Library of Congress, Baine News Service LC-DIG-ggbain-20361.*

Sturge, a medical doctor, missionary and poet, began establishing missions for the Japanese in California in 1886, supported by the Presbyterian Church. He traveled to Yokohama, Japan, shortly after attending the 1910 dedication ceremony for the Wintersburg Mission and traveled extensively through Asia. In recognition of his dedication, Sturge was presented a book by his

Japanese colleagues, *The Spirit of Japan*, in 1903. It includes a biographical sketch, a collection of his poetry and classic examples of Japanese literature, such as the *Song of Urashima*. The book includes an inscription that it was added to the U.S. Library of Congress by Reverend Joseph K. Inazawa, the first official clergyman for the Wintersburg Mission in 1910.

A monument for Sturge at the Colma, California Japanese Cemetery notes that he established fourteen Japanese missions on the Pacific Coast by the time of his death in 1934, including the Wintersburg Mission. At the time that *The Spirit of Japan* was published in 1903, there were four missions noted in the book: San Francisco, Los Angeles, Salinas and Watsonville. By the next year, the Wintersburg Mission was founded. Among the documents in the present-day Wintersburg Church archives are ledger notes of Sturge's own financial donations to the Wintersburg Mission building fund, one in 1911 for $120, and a letter from him in 1919 to the Wintersburg trustees calling Reverend Nakamura to another mission effort in Sacramento, California.

The cenotaph in Colma notes that Sturge gave "his very homes for our use" in San Francisco and San Mateo. His work with the Japanese prompted the Emperor Meiji to award Sturge with the Order of the Rising Sun. He died in 1934, the year the second church building opened in Wintersburg Village.

Charles Furuta supported the mission effort from its inception, becoming one of the mission's first trustees and, later, an elder. A notation from the Santa Ana First Presbyterian Church in 1912 entrusts him with a "birthday offering of Sunday School to the Japanese Presbyterian Mission, Wintersburg." Furuta is noted in a "subscriber's list" as contributing significant amounts compared to other Japanese donors, which in addition to his later donation of more land, made him one of the mission's largest benefactors. Furuta continued to care for the mission property, providing additional land for the 1934 church building, as the mission grew to become the heart of coastal Orange County's Japanese community.

The early 1900s church-building effort also was noticed and supported by the local European American pioneer community. Among those who contributed to the mission-building fund are some of Huntington Beach's early families: George W. Moore, M.C. Cole, E.H. Darling, S.J. Burgess, the Cranes, the Clemonses, the Chaffees, the Woodingtons, the Farrars, the Hearns, the Nicholses, the Blaylocks, the Shaffers and the Reeds. Early businesses that supported the Japanese Mission fund were the Holly Sugar Factory, Huntington Beach National Bank, California Vegetable Union,

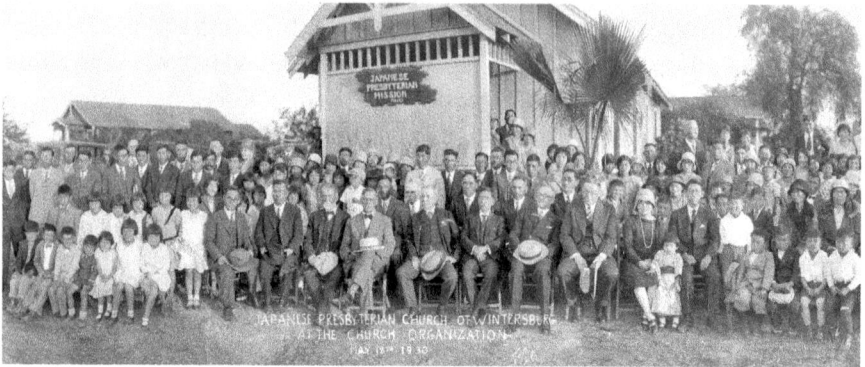

Wintersburg Japanese Presbyterian Mission, circa 1930, twenty years after the mission's construction. Charles Furuta is in the second row, above the name "Wintersburg." *Wintersburg Presbyterian Church.*

Pacific Vegetable Company and Halsell Drug Company. The mission building was also supported by the Wintersburg ME Church Women's Missionary Society, Women's Missionary Society of Orange County, First Presbyterian Church of Santa Ana and the Westminster Presbyterian Church, as well as clergy members from around the county.

Growth During the Great Depression

"This Mission was opened on the Christmas season of 1904," reads a faded, typed history of the Wintersburg Mission, written in 1930 by Reverend Kenji Kikuchi. It was twenty-six years after its founding, the year the mission was formally recognized as an organized Presbyterian Church and the first year of the Great Depression.

By then, the mission was already being described as "one of the oldest Japanese churches in Southern California." Ten Japanese pastors had served the mission by 1930, and it had become the "only center of the Japanese community in this vicinity." In Orange County, the Anaheim Japanese ME Church had served a smaller population of Japanese immigrants, about a fifth of the size of Wintersburg.

At the time of the founding, the official census of Orange County did not yet include a population count for Huntington Beach. It wasn't until the 1910 census that Huntington Beach reached a notable population of 815 (after incorporating in 1909).

PROGRAM

SUNDAY, DECEMBER 9th, 1934
2:00 P. M.

MR. N. TAMURA, Presiding

Prelude . . . . Miss Toshiko Furuta
Hymn (144)
Scripture Reading, Prayer . . . . Rev. J. J. Nakamura
Vocal Solo—"Open the Gate of the Temple" . . . . Miss Mary Chino

30th Anniversary Speeches . . . . { Mr. C. M. Furuta, Elder
{ Mr. Lionard Miyawaki

    Rep. Westminster Presby. Church . . . . Mr. O. B. Byran, Elder
    First Pastor of the Mission . . . . Rev. B. H. Terasawa

Hymn (530)
Words of Dedication . . . . Rev. K. Kikuchi
Dedication Prayer . . . . Rev. R. B. McAulay, D.D.
Congratulatory Greetings—

    Rep. Sunday School . . . . Miss Kazuko Furuta
    Rep. Christian Endeavor . . . . Mr. Roy Kanegae
    Rep. the Church . . . . Mr. K. Ishii, Elder

Violin Solo—"Romance"—By Johan S. Svendsen . . . . Miss Sumi Akiyama
Congratulatory Greetings, Representing—

    Japanese Association of Smeltzer . . . . Mr. H. Tamura
    Talbert Japanese School . . . . Mr. H. Okada
    Orange County J. Y. P. A. . . . . Mr. C. Nishizu
    Japanese Presbyterian Churches . . . . Rev. T. Horikoshi
    Japanese Church Federation . . . . Rev. Y. Yamaga
    Presbyterian Churches of Orange County . . . . Rev. O. S. McFarland
    Board of National Mission . . . . Rev. P. F. Payne, D.D.
    Board of Church Extension of Los Angeles Presbytery . . Rev. G. W. Wadsworth, D.D.

Congratulatory Telegram . . . . Mr. K. Hokoyama
Public Recognition for Service Rendered
Report of Treasurer . . . . Mr. S. Kanno, Treasurer
Report of the New Building—Chairman of Building Committee . . . Rev. T. H. Walker
Dedication Offering
Doxology—Praise God
Benediction . . . . Rev. J. G. Klene, D.D.

Group Picture and Motion Pictures to be Taken

Refreshments

The Church is located ½ mile west of Huntington Beach Boulevard on Wintersburg Road

Wintersburg Japanese Presbyterian Church program for the ceremony
recognizing its official organization as a church, 1934. *Furuta family collection.*

By 1930, the Wintersburg Japanese Presbyterian Mission had outgrown its
original wooden sanctuary and began contemplating a new church building
effort. The population of Orange County's Japanese Americans had grown.

The Reverend Kenji Kikuchi became the pastor in 1926, having completed
seminary in Japan and theology studies at Princeton. He writes about the

"situation of the Japanese people in Orange County," a population of two thousand, "most of them farmers...about 350 families."

Kikuchi's historical summary noted there were about 150 Japanese families in the immediate vicinity of Wintersburg: "Most of them are dry chili pepper farmers—they raise half [a] million dollars a year production from peppers. Also there are three (big) gold fish farms owned by our church members." These would have been the goldfish farms of Charles Furuta, Tsurumatsu Asari and Henry Akiyama.

During a 1981 oral history interview, Kikuchi remembered when he first learned about Wintersburg. "After coming to California, I found a Japanese community I never knew existed and which very strongly needed a leader and pastor," recalls Kikuchi. "I felt very deeply about such a mission."

"The Japanese people or community wanted to bring in a minister who spoke English, who knew the United States. So we started," explained Kikuchi. "The community relation was very close, more family like, and I had to help out the children, calling for a doctor or taking a patient to the hospital. Nobody could help but the minister, and he was in the best position to help out."

"So many young people came to this small Wintersburg church in Orange County," continued Reverend Kikuchi, eighty-three years old

Wintersburg Japanese Presbyterian Church at the dedication of its second house of worship in 1934. *Wintersburg Presbyterian Church.*

at the time of his interview. He described the original redwood mission building as "very old."

"It was built in 1910, and my predecessor as pastor was Reverend Junzo Nakamura. He was a very good leader," recalled Kikuchi. "It was kind of a painstaking job for a minister because it was not a formally organized church. We had to start from nothing, and we had to teach many things."

When Kikuchi arrived, Nakamura had already left for a ministry in San Diego, and it was clear the Wintersburg Mission needed support: "The corner lot where the church was located was overgrown with dry weeds. Then about a hundred Japanese people, *Issei* and *Nisei*, came to the area so I was deeply determined to take care of them."

About two years after Kikuchi arrived at the mission, it organized officially as a church—the Japanese Presbyterian Church of Wintersburg.

"We planned a new building because the number of Sunday school children increased, and we used to go around the Talbert area to get the children in my Model-T Ford [laughter]—about nineteen children in an open car—and I drove around the surrounding farm land to get the Sunday school children here," continued Reverend Kikuchi.

BUILDING A NEW CHURCH DURING THE DEPRESSION YEARS

The funds for the 1934 church building were raised—and, almost lost—during the Great Depression.

"We collected donations little by little. First, we deposited the money in the Huntington Beach Bank, a state bank. But in the prime of the Depression, the deposits were frozen," remembers Kikuchi. "Charlie's [Ishii] father and I ran to the Huntington Beach Bank, but the bank was closed. We almost felt like crying. But, later, when we fixed pews in the church, we could draw our deposit from the bank after the arrangement by the government. In this way, we collected small amounts of money little by little."

Kikuchi stayed on as pastor at the Wintersburg Japanese Presbyterian Church until 1936, after the construction of the 1934 church building. In 1942, he and his wife, Yoshi, were evacuated to the Colorado River Relocation Center at Poston, Arizona.

Kikuchi's interviewer for his 1982 oral history remarks that he "radiated a warmth and good cheer rarely seen by me in any other people I have known."

"So for ten years I never got tired, never became disappointed, and thoroughly enjoyed myself," Kikuchi recalls of his time at the Japanese Presbyterian Church in Wintersburg. "Most of the people enjoyed our lives with us like we were a family."

Chapter 8

GOLDFISH ON
WINTERSBURG AVENUE

O ne of the remarkable oral histories conducted in 1982 for Orange County's Japanese American Project captured the history and memories of Clarence Iwao Nishizu, a congregant of the Wintersburg Japanese Presbyterian Mission.

Nishizu, a *Nisei* born in Los Angeles in 1910, rose from farming to become a prominent land broker. He also was a passionate advocate for civil rights and the preservation of Japanese American history. He was the cofounder of several Japanese American Citizens' League chapters, the first Japanese American selected as the foreman of the Orange County Grand Jury, active in the Redress campaign that led to passage of the Civil Liberties Act of 1988, awarded an honorary doctorate of humane letters from California State University–Fullerton and led the fundraising campaign that built the Orange County Agricultural and Nikkei Heritage Museum at California State University's Fullerton Arboretum.

The author of Nishizu's 2006 obituary for the *Orange County Register* described him as a "gentle man with an impish twinkle in his eye and an air of naiveté about him." But the author added that "looks can be deceiving" when recalling Nishizu's tenacity, wit and drive.

Nishizu's accounts of Wintersburg are remarkably detailed and revealing of his wry sense of humor. His oral history is one of several that describe the three goldfish farms of Orange County, all of which originated in the Wintersburg Village. One distinct recollection was about the Asari Goldfish Hatchery.

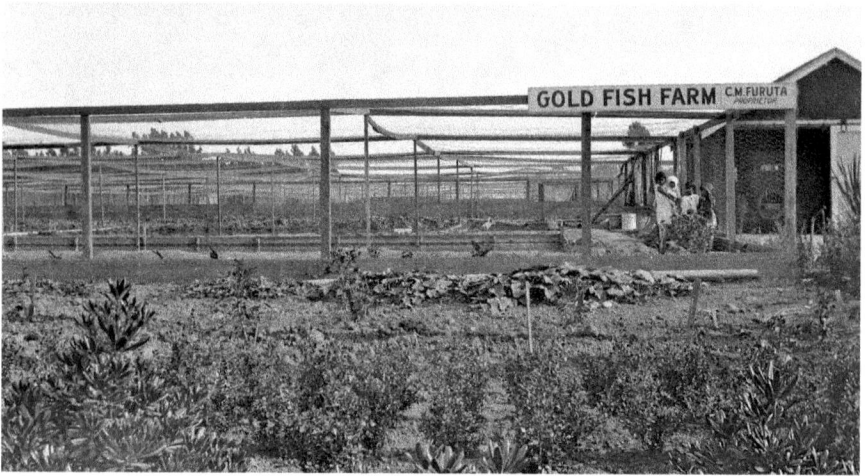

C.M. Furuta Gold Fish Farm, circa 1920s. *Furuta family collection.*

Asari—reported to be one of the first Japanese to arrive in Orange County in the late 1800s—opened a goldfish hatchery in Wintersburg in the early 1920s, post–World War I, after seeing the successful results of Charles Furuta and Henry Akiyama. Asari was already a successful farmer, farming acres of sugar beets and alfalfa. He was considered a community leader, supporting the establishment of the Japanese Presbyterian Mission in Wintersburg as well as Orange County's first Buddhist church.

Asari had "made enough money to purchase forty acres in Wintersburg, where he started farming vegetables," recalls Nishizu. "His son, Harley, has told me that at the time his family moved to Wintersburg, the area was full of tules and open fields."

Asari also opened one of the first grocery stores in Wintersburg, later owned by Gunjiro Tashima—located off what are today Lyndon Lane and Warner Avenue, across the street from the Japanese Presbyterian Mission. Harley Asari worked with his father at the goldfish farm.

"SOMETHING LIVELY JUMPING UP AND DOWN"

"I recall an incident that occurred years ago that involved the Asari fish," recalled Nishizu. "One evening I was driving on Stanton Boulevard, now

Stopped by the side of the road in Wintersburg, circa 1913. *Furuta family collection.*

Beach Boulevard. About a mile south of Stanton, where there was a bend in the highway, I noticed that many cars had stopped on the road."

Soon I could see thousands of something lively jumping up and down on the pavement," relays Nishizu. "The cars had stopped because nobody wanted to run over the beautiful goldfish strewn all over the road. I stopped my car and went to find out what happened."

"Apparently Harley Asari was hauling the goldfish on his Dodge pickup truck, whose rear loading space was covered on the top and screened on the side, when he was involved in an accident," continues Nishizu. "Harley was a young lad then who was conscientiously helping his father, and I felt very sorry that the accident had happened to him. I wanted to pick up the goldfish and retrieve them for him, but the fish were too elusive."

The goldfish farms survived more than one upheaval. There was the earthquake of 1933, causing many to "tent out" until the aftershakes were over. During the nonstop heavy rains of 1938, it was reported in the *Huntington Beach News* that "Harley Asari's goldfish hatchery lost several thousand valuable goldfish" when the Santa Ana River flooded.

And Then, World War II

There is a photograph of goldfish farmer Harley Asari at a Denver foundry. Harley, along with most Wintersburg and Huntington Beach residents of

Harley Asari at a Denver-area foundry during World War II. *Federal Depository Library Program.*

Japanese ancestry, was evacuated to the Colorado River Relocation Center at Poston, Arizona.

The photograph shows Harley working with another evacuee in 1944, during the war. The photograph also was used in a Department of the Interior War Relocation Authority (WRA) publication, *New Neighbors Among Us*, which reported on the progress of relocated Japanese Americans.

In order to be granted "leave clearance," the publication explains that Harley—born in Wintersburg and a graduate of Huntington Beach High School—would have completed a questionnaire created by intelligence officials for the WRA. His name was submitted for intelligence agency review to prove he was a "loyal American citizen," before he was allowed to leave for Colorado.

The *New Neighbors Among Us* pamphlet—while mainly propaganda to justify relocation—notes that after the war, Japanese Americans "scattered to most of the states outside the excluded Pacific coast area. Some regions have seemed more favorable and have drawn greater numbers, but at no point do they approach the concentrations which were found in the 'Little Tokyos' of Los Angeles and other West Coast cities, or in the irrigated valleys of inland California before evacuation."

Remarkably, the farms of Wintersburg's three goldfish farmers were waiting for them to return to Orange County and start their lives again.

AFTER THE WAR

Wintersburg ultimately was annexed into the City of Huntington Beach in 1957. The Huntington Beach City Council minutes of March 7, 1960, show a business license approval for the Asari Goldfish Hatchery, Inc., 8741

Wintersburg Avenue, "for the business of Raising Tropical Fish, Goldfish and Distributing Pet Supplies."

By May of that year, the city had enacted zone changes as part of an overall general plan, zoning the property as residential. When the family came before the planning commission to obtain a variance to continue their goldfish hatchery operations, commissioners noted that the Asari goldfish farm was a "longtime established operation with a profitable tax base for the City" and allowed the variance. The Asari Goldfish Hatchery had been in operation almost forty years.

The Asari property—in the northwest area of present-day Warner (Wintersburg) Avenue and Magnolia (Cannery) Street near the 405 Freeway—eventually succumbed to urbanization and was rezoned as residential land by the City of Huntington Beach in March 1964.

At the same meeting, the large Chikasawa farm—located at present-day Warner Avenue and Edwards Street—was rezoned residential. During the last half of the twentieth century, the goldfish and agricultural farms were disappearing and the urban landscape moving in—with the exception of the Charles and Yukiko Furuta farm in the former Wintersburg Village.

THE GOLDFISH FARMERS

Goldfish had been bred in captivity for more than 1,500 years and reportedly made their way into the United States by at least the mid-1800s. Though there is a long history of goldfish farming in Asia, it was still a fairly new enterprise for America. With the rise of chain stores with pet departments, the small, glittering fish delighted the American public and ignited a trend that remains popular today.

Interviewed in 1982, Henry Kiyomi Akiyama confirmed there were only three major goldfish farms in Orange County, all starting in Wintersburg: the C.M. Furuta Gold Fish Farm (Charles Mitsuji Furuta), the Asari Gold Fish Farm (Tsurumatsu Asari) and the mammoth Pacific Goldfish Farm (Henry Kiyomi Akiyama)—all three farmers supported the Wintersburg Japanese Presbyterian Mission.

Charles and Yukiko Furuta, along with Henry and Masuko Akiyama (Yukiko's sister), had worked and lived in a large house on the Cole Ranch, located off present-day Warner Avenue and Gothard Street in the area of

Above: Etsuko, Toshiko and baby Grace Furuta at the C.M. Furuta Gold Fish Farm, 1928. *Furuta family collection.*

Left: Yukiko and Charles Furuta with their son Raymond and Masako and Henry Akiyama, circa 1914. *Furuta family collection.*

today's Ocean View High School in Huntington Beach. By working the Cole Ranch, the Furutas and Akiyamas saved money that allowed them to develop independent enterprises.

By the 1920s, Charles Furuta and his brother-in-law, Henry Akiyama, had tried goldfish ponds on the Furuta farm. Akiyama recalled some of his relatives in Japan had raised *koi* (carp), and he had watched their farming

Yukiko Furuta on the porch of the Cole Ranch in Wintersburg. *Furuta family collection.*

practices before leaving for America. An experimental goldfish pond proved the fish multiplied easily. Akiyama went on to try more ponds on the Cole Ranch in Wintersburg.

THE FIRST GOLDFISH PONDS

The Furutas moved back to their own property around 1920 and began working the farm. (The family report that the first pond may have been ·started there before they moved back into their home.) Henry and Masuko Akiyama also moved back to the Furuta farm, living in the former Terahata home, a small house Charles Furuta had moved to his property. The goldfish ponds on the Furuta property became the first commercial goldfish ponds attempted in Orange County.

There were only a handful of goldfish businesses across the United States. By 1928, the Orange County City Directory shows a few stores in Santa Ana and Costa Mesa were selling a variety of birds, goldfish and aquariums, among them the Orana Bird and Goldfish Company in Santa Ana, advertised as "the pioneer bird man of Orange County."

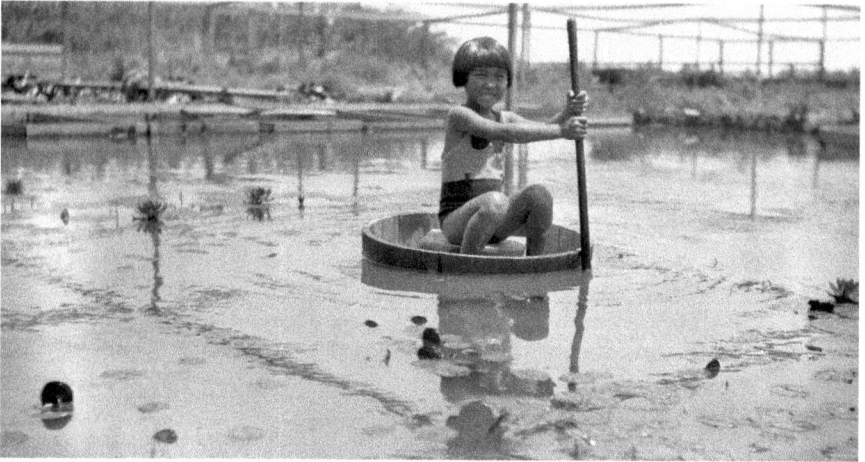

Grace Furuta with her "raft" on a goldfish pond, circa 1935. *Furuta family collection.*

The *Issei* farmers took barrels of goldfish by pickup truck to Orange County, Long Beach and Los Angeles. Later, goldfish were shipped in barrel containers by train to buyers around the country.

THE C.M. FURUTA GOLD FISH FARM

Charles Furuta increased the pond acreage at his farm, eventually covering over three acres of the five-acre property. The rest of the acreage was taken up by the Furuta home, Wintersburg Japanese Presbyterian Mission complex, food and flower crops and some small livestock.

The Furuta Gold Fish Farm ponds contained a variety of species, indicating local goldfish farmers were specializing to accommodate growing market demands for the exotic fish. In addition to the more common Comets, there were Black Moors, Fantails, Shubunkin and Nymphs. A freshwater well on the Furuta farm and a network of irrigation piping kept the pond acreage filled.

The C.M. Furuta Gold Fish Farm continued to operate up until World War II. President of the Smeltzer Japanese Association and an American resident for forty-one years, Charles Furuta was incarcerated along with other community and religious leaders.

He was taken first to Tajunga "Tuna Canyon" Detention Station in Los Angeles County. His daughter Etsuko remembered in a 2013 oral history

Furuta Gold Fish Farm. *Furuta family collection.*

that she had to talk to her father through a wire fence. Charles's wife, Yukiko, said in her 1982 oral history interview that he instructed the family to stay together and do as they were told.

Charles Furuta was later moved to the Department of Justice's Lordsburg, New Mexico "enemy alien" center while his family was sent to the Colorado River Relocation Center near Poston, Arizona. After more than a year's separation, he joined them in 1943 at Poston, Camp 1, Block 12. Their barrack cell was located next to their then twenty-nine-year-old son, Raymond; his wife, Martha; and, in 1944, the couple's newborn, Kenneth. Henry and Masuko Akiyama, and their son, Joe, also were next door.

During their years of incarceration, the Furuta family rented their house to a Caucasian family they knew and asked that they maintain the ponds. Martha Furuta, interviewed by her son Norman, said they originally thought their time in the relocation center would be short in duration. As time passed, the cost of irrigating the ponds and the uncertainty of how long the Furuta family would be incarcerated evidently led to a decision by the tenants to stop pond maintenance. Upon the Furuta's return from Poston, Arizona, their home was in good—although unkempt—condition, the farm overgrown and the ponds filled with silt. However, unlike other families leaving incarceration, the Furutas owned their property and had a home to which they could return.

Water lilies on the Furuta farm, circa 2000. *Furuta family collection.*

The Furutas did not restore the ponds for goldfish. Instead, they recovered the lily flower roots—still alive—and began farming water lilies.

One of the additions on the Furuta barn includes shallow sorting troughs, which were filled with water to keep the sweet pea flowers fresh after they were cut and prepared for market. After harvesting, the water lilies were stored in a large, walk-in icebox inside the barn. Norman Furuta—grandson of Charles and Yukiko Furuta and a graduate of Huntington Beach High School—recalls preparing cut water lilies as "a pretty labor-intensive process."

"Each flower had to be 'waxed' by my parents [Raymond and Martha Furuta] by dripping a candle around the center of the flower while it was open," explained Norman Furuta. "If this was not done, the lily completely closes when the sun sets, and doesn't open again until morning."

Norman Furuta notes his family's farm was "to the family's knowledge, the only source of cut water lilies in the United States during the last half of the 20th century. We were aware of other commercial sellers of water lily plants, but my father [Raymond Furuta] wasn't aware of anyone else producing cut water lilies for commercial use."

This crop, along with sweet pea flowers, proved to be a successful enterprise for the Furuta family, after World War II through the end of the twentieth century, creating what Yukiko Furuta recalled was "a good life."

While most Orange County farmers grew food crops needed for kitchens around the country, the Furuta farm cultivated beauty in the form of *nishikigoi*—the "living jewels" in the ponds—and the exotic flowers wanted for our homes.

PACIFIC GOLDFISH FARM

Henry Kiyomi Akiyama's Pacific Goldfish Farm—an idea originating from the Furuta farm—expanded at the Cole Ranch, a short distance west on Wintersburg Avenue, and later to a forty-acre site in the nearby community of Westminster.

Born in 1888 to Somonji and Wai Akiyama in Nagano, Japan, Akiyama traveled to America from Japan in 1904, when he was sixteen years old. Like Charles Furuta, he first worked in the lumber industry in Washington State, making his way to Southern California by 1907. And like many Japanese immigrants in Orange County, his first job was cutting celery.

Aerial of Pacific Goldfish Farm, circa 1940s. *California State University Fullerton, Center for Oral and Public History, AK1751.*

Aerial of Pacific Goldfish Farm at Goldenwest and Bolsa Streets, circa 1955. *Orange County Archives.*

By the 1920s, he was raising goldfish full time. Akiyama was Charles Furuta's friend and his brother-in-law, marrying Yukiko Yajima Furuta's sister, Masuko, in 1914. He had seen a photograph of Masuko in the Furuta home, and Yukiko, thinking it was a good match, wrote home to Japan asking her to come to America.

The discovery of oil in Huntington Beach led some local farmers to sell off all or part of their land and retire from farming. The Cole family sold part of the Cole Ranch land during that time but agreed to partner with

Interior of Pacific Goldfish Farm, circa 1950s. *Courtesy of Akiyama family, California State University Fullerton, Center for Oral and Public History, AK1757.*

Akiyama on a goldfish pond in 1919. Akiyama had farmed the Cole Ranch land since 1910 and developed a strong relationship with the family. He continued to farm the Cole Ranch land while cultivating goldfish.

A significant turning point came when Akiyama decided to lease land in Westminster to expand the goldfish business. Crawfish were invading the ponds on the Cole Ranch property, eating the fish. He needed land where he could create new ponds and a covered hatchery.

Akiyama was lent money by the Cole family for the Westminster land, which he planned to lease for ten to twenty years and eventually pay off the land price. This time, his goldfish venture succeeded in a big way.

Akiyama's interpreter for his 1982 interview explains, "When [he] started this goldfish business, he didn't have much of an idea on how to make a pond or how to make a drain, so his business was not so great a success." His son, Joseph, recalled the earliest days of goldfish farming in a 1980s *Los Angeles Times* article, watching his father load "an old pickup truck with barrels of goldfish and driving up to Los Angeles to sell his swimming rainbows door to door at pet shops."

Akiyama discovered that the "most important thing in raising goldfish is the food and the water." He described tasting the fish food himself, using it only "if he thought it tasted good." His homemade concoctions were made with wheat, fish meal, shrimp powder and locally caught anchovies.

Akiyama began hiring Caucasians to make the deliveries (these employees later faced suspicion and discrimination during World War II). First delivering fish to Long Beach and Los Angeles, Akiyama later shipped fish to Oregon, Seattle, the Midwest and New Zealand. The Pacific Goldfish Farm used catalogs to advertise its glittery product, shipping the fish around the country in barrels via railroad express.

It is estimated there were 100,000 to 200,000 fish by the time World War II started. An *Issei*, Akiyama was prohibited from buying land after California's Alien Land Laws of 1913 and 1923. Faced with evacuation to Arizona, Akiyama was able to put the farm lease in the name of his American-born son, Joseph. His Caucasian employees continued managing the farm while the Akiyama family was incarcerated at the Colorado River Relocation Center at Poston, Arizona. However, when more men left for war, the farm maintenance suffered.

While at Poston, Akiyama—then fifty-four—raised *koi*. An irrigation canal was dug through the desert to bring in Colorado River water, and Akiyama, along with other internees, made nets to catch the carp. In the sweltering Arizona sun, the *koi* may have brought a measure of peace in an

Aerial of Pacific Goldfish Farm, circa 1958. *Courtesy of Akiyama family and California State University Fullerton, Center for Oral and Public History, AK 1751.*

unreal situation. Akiyama received nineteen dollars per month to cultivate the fish and teach others the business.

After World War II, Akiyama cleared his ponds of weeds and frogs and began including *koi* at the farm in Westminster, encouraged by Japanese students learning the fishing business in America. The popularity of *koi*—*nishikigoi* or "brocaded carp"—took off and the business thrived.

Asked by his oral history interviewer if the Orange County farms were the center of goldfish production in the United States, Akiyama confirmed they were, with smaller groups in Indiana and Chicago. A 1963 historical reference for Orange County reports that "at the time of inception of Mr. Akiyama's business, there were no more than twelve fish farms in all the United States, and today his is the largest goldfish farm west of the Mississippi." The Pacific Goldfish Farm—worth around $1 million in 1963—prompted Westminster to promote itself as the "Goldfish Capital of the World."

By the latter half of the twentieth century, the construction of the 405 Freeway and urbanization erased the Pacific Goldfish Farm and the Asari Goldfish Hatchery. As of the beginning of 2014, the last remaining goldfish farm not lost to development is the Furuta Gold Fish Farm property—on Warner Avenue in the former Wintersburg Village—where the first goldfish pond in Orange County began.

Chapter 9

THE MARRIAGE THAT
MADE HEADLINES

Imagine having to explain your marriage on the front page of metropolitan newspapers across the country. This was the case for the Wintersburg Japanese Presbyterian Mission's first minister and his bride, Reverend Joseph Kenichi Inazawa and Miss Kate Alice Goodman, in the winter of 1910.

Neither was a wealthy land baron, railroad tycoon or royalty. Nor were they notorious for questionable politics or crimes. Both were in their forties and had known each other for some time. Theirs was a marriage between a respected clergyman and a longtime church worker, a marriage that should have received only a quiet announcement in the society section of the local newspaper.

He was Japanese. She was Caucasian. And their groundbreaking marriage triggered intense public fascination of the kind we see in today's celebrity media. It was a public spotlight that would make anyone want to run for the hills—or maybe for the peatlands of Wintersburg.

REVEREND INAZAWA

Born in the Iwami Province in Japan in 1863, Reverend Inazawa arrived in the United States in the late 1800s after attending seminary in Tokyo. He performed his postgraduate work at the San Francisco Theological Seminary, graduating with the class of 1894. The *San Francisco Call* reported that he was one of two Japanese seminary graduates ordained at the annual Presbytery convocation in April 1896 (the other, J. Okuno).

Prior to his work in Los Angeles, Inazawa worked as an itinerant Presbyterian clergyman throughout California, including in San Francisco, Salinas, Watsonville and Santa Cruz. The Japanese Presbyterian Church of Salinas, California (Lincoln Avenue) credits Inazawa with the establishment of the original mission in 1898, meeting above a blacksmith's shop. By 1902, he had negotiated a land purchase for the mission. The present-day church's website describes Inazawa as "a rare person of integrity."

Reverend Inazawa's biography for the San Francisco Theological Seminary alumni indicates he helped compile the selected poems, artwork and addresses for *Spirit of Japan* for Dr. Ernest Adolphus Sturge—a supporter of Japanese mission work on the Pacific Coast—and translated a number of Presbyterian publications.

By 1902—the same year Presbyterian clergy began meeting Japanese farmers in Wintersburg—the Japanese Presbyterian Church of Los Angeles was forming. Church records indicate that Reverend Inazawa arrived in 1905, developing the Los Angeles group into a "regular Presbyterian congregation." The *Los Angeles Herald* wrote Reverend Inazawa was fluent in English and the scriptures and that he had been "actively identified with Presbyterian missions and churches" in the United States for twenty years.

KATE ALICE GOODMAN

Kate Goodman was originally from New York. She was a University of Chicago graduate and was described by the *New York Tribune* as coming from a "good New York family." She is reported working for nine years to help establish Japanese missions in New York, Chicago and Los Angeles. Prior to the marriage, she had been teaching at a Japanese school in Moneta (Gardena, California).

She and Reverend Inazawa met while "thrown together" teaching Bible classes, and they formed an "attachment."

Reports of the engagement between Reverend Inazawa and Kate Goodman in the spring of 1909 made news across the country and in other countries, as far away as New Zealand. The April 13, 1909 *Washington Herald* writing from the nation's capital was blunt in its headline, "Japanese to Wed White Girl." The *Olean Times* (New York) reported that "Mr. Inazawa was greatly surprised when he learned his secret had leaked out but freely acknowledged the truth of the report." Like anyone today wisely trying to avoid the paparazzi, Reverend Inazawa told the newspaper that no date had been set for the wedding ceremony.

In California, the *Los Angeles Herald* reported in 1910 that "Cupid was sent scampering away until she could read and investigate the advisability and probable consequences of such a union." At forty-two years old, Kate Goodman was not prone to the flowery language that the *Herald* used when writing about the two.

Knowing there was more than a little interest about their marriage, Kate Goodman prepared a written statement that was delivered to the *Los Angeles Herald* on February 23, as she and Reverend Inazawa left for Laguna, New Mexico, to be married. The *Herald* reported her as telling friends, "Say for me that I am happy. I don't care what the world thinks. Joseph and I are happy."

Goodman's written statement can easily be interpreted into twenty-first-century language as "We've got this. Everything is fine." There is a veiled admonishment to the media about sensationalizing the marriage.

Goodman writes:

> *When the marriage of two persons of humble circumstances is given space on the first page of a metropolitan daily the only inference to be drawn is that such marriage is regarded as sensational in character. When the hitherto law abiding members of a community leave the state in order to consummate a legal marriage, a decent regard for the opinions of mankind would seem to warrant a word of explanation…*
>
> *It has been suggested to me that this marriage may be regarded by some as a piece of emotionalism unsupported by the judgment. Such is very far from the truth. In fact neither of us has any startling record of rash acts committed in the past and after 40 years of age character should be somewhat settled, it would seem…In the choice of a husband I certainly have not been unduly precipitous…I have given to the subject the most continuous concentrated, serious and honest thought of my life.*

Goodman concludes her statement with a Tennyson quote, Genevieve to King Arthur: "We needs must love the highest when we see it." As with the leaked engagement news, Goodman's statement was included in newspapers around the country—often on the front page.

A 1910 edition of the *Pacific Presbyterian* announced the marriage: "Rev. J.K. Inazawa and Miss Kate A. Goodman were united in marriage last week

Los Angeles Herald front-page story on the marriage of Reverend Inazawa and Miss Kate Goodman, February 27, 1910. *Chronicling America, Library of Congress.*

in a very quiet way. The engagement was announced some time ago." The announcement concludes, "This new relation ought to increase the efficiency of both, as the promise is that one shall chase a thousand and two put ten thousand to flight."

IN WINTERSBURG

At the time of the marriage, President Taft had been in office a year, and Washington was embroiled in the congressional investigation of the Pinchot-Ballinger controversy. News about the Inazawas joined articles about Theodore Roosevelt's hunting exploits in Africa and the Empress Eugénie's last days on the French Riviera. New Mexico and Arizona had yet to be officially admitted into the Union. Railroad tycoon James J. Hill was chastising Americans for living beyond their means, while John D. Rockefeller announced he would donate a billion dollars to charity over his lifetime.

The Inazawa marriage—along with the features on Roosevelt or Empress Eugénie—does not seem to have had the same buzz in Wintersburg as in metropolitan society. More likely, the diverse population was focused on the hard work of farming and creating a community.

In his 1982 oral history interview, Wintersburg goldfish farmer Henry Kiyomi Akiyama mentions Reverend Inazawa. His is the only oral history found that mentions the couple. Akiyama said Reverend Inazawa "was the first reverend after the missionary building was built here and he was married to a *hakujin* (Caucasian)." And that's it. Seventy-two years later, it was a simple observation.

A PERMANENCY OF HAPPINESS

The Inazawas had many supporters. The national newspaper the *Christian Work and the Evangelist* included a news item in 1910 about the Inazawas shortly after their marriage:

"In Laguna, New Mexico, has occurred a marriage of the Reverend Joseph Kenichi Inazawa and Miss Kate Goodman. He is pastor of a Japanese Presbyterian Church and she is a mission worker. He is 46 and she is slightly his junior," reports the newspaper, explaining that Miss Goodman had to defend the choice of her husband.

"Anyone who considers her husband is all right biologically, anthropologically, sociologically, psychologically, and theologically ought to be happy!" the newspaper continues. "Many of our girls only stop to inquire if a fellow is financially right. It is better to trust to induction and deduction every time!"

The *Hawaiian Star* newspaper in Honolulu reporting from Los Angeles in March 1910 notes, "The bride is 45. She is highly connected in the East. Strange to relate there was no apparent opposition on their part to her choice of a husband and the marriage has general religious sanction in this City. Inazawa stands high among the ministers of all denominations."

A few years after the Inazawas' marriage, Neeta Marquis wrote about them in a 1913 article, "Interracial Amity in Los Angeles, Personal Observations on the Life of the Japanese in Los Angeles." Marquis, a California writer, authored books about Presbyterian history and art, as well as works such as *Earth's Story of Evolution: From Cosmic Dust to the Present Age*. In the article, Marquis writes:

> *Between two and three years ago, when the native pastor of the Japanese Presbyterian Church, Joseph K. Inazawa, a scholarly and interesting man of highly pleasing personality, was married to an American lady, a reception was tendered the couple at the home of one of the prominent American ministers, and the American and Japanese friends of the two mingled as guests. The alliance caused considerable comment at the time, the general sentiment of the American public not personally acquainted with the principals being, of course, opposed to the union.*
>
> *Mrs. Inazawa, then Miss Kate Goodman, a Christian woman of independent character, experienced in teaching and normal school work, formerly a student at the University of Chicago, had for nine years worked among and studied the Japanese in New York, Chicago and Los Angeles. As a concession to public opinion, she published a statement defining her attitude on the matter of her marriage. The statement...was a clear, finished, logical and sane production.*

Marquis writes about meeting with Mrs. Inazawa and finding her to be "a thoroly [*sic*] normal American woman of the broadly intellectual type, possest [*sic*] of a delightful sense of humor and more than willing to answer the questions I was eager to ask her." Kate Inazawa is reported as telling Marquis that "she would be glad for the American public to know that over two years of life as the wife of a Japanese Christian gentleman had in no particular altered the personal attitude toward inter-racial marriage which she stated at the time of her union with Mr. Inazawa."

Marquis summarizes that the Inazawa marriage is successful because the "husband and wife are one in ideals, aims and spiritual outlook" and that "a permanency of happiness can be expected."

THE WINTERSBURG MISSION

Reverend Inazawa held the first official service in the newly constructed Wintersburg Japanese Presbyterian Mission in 1910, during his first year of marriage to Kate Goodman. The couple would have been the first to live in the manse adjacent to the mission, also constructed in 1910.

They were undoubtedly breaking with state law. California banned interracial marriage in 1850, until the 1948 California Supreme Court case *Perez v. Sharp* ruled that the anti-miscegenation statute violated the Fourteenth Amendment to the United States Constitution. California then became the first state to repeal an anti-miscegenation law since Ohio in 1887.

New Mexico—where the Inazawas traveled to marry—repealed anti-miscegenation laws in 1866. Twelve years after Joseph and Kate Inazawa married, the United States Congress passed the Cable Act, which retroactively stripped the citizenship of any U.S. citizen who married "an alien ineligible for citizenship." This law would have applied to Kate Alice Goodman Inazawa. It was not until 1967—fifty-seven years after the Inazawa marriage—that the United States Supreme Court ruled the state bans still in place violated the Fourteenth Amendment to the U.S. Constitution, in *Loving v. Virginia*.

The celebration in Wintersburg Village for the Taishō emperor, circa 1911, was attended by both the Japanese and Caucasian residents in Wintersburg. Charles Furuta is standing in front of wagon. *Furuta family collection.*

Marquis' article about the Inazawas was published in July 1913, two months after the California legislature in Sacramento passed the Alien Land Law, which prohibited Japanese from owning property. Nevertheless, she writes with optimism about relations with the Japanese in Southern California:

> *Knowing that others all over Southern California are having similar experiences in both the business and the social world—very especially among the agricultural classes owning and working the great celery fields of Orange County, where the entire countryside accepted the invitation of the Japanese to join them in their celebration of the Emperor's last birthday. I am convinced that a feeling of better understanding is graciously winning its way in the land where the dragon and the eagle are destined if not quite to "lie down together," at least to eat together in peace.*

Chapter 10

THE SMELTZER
FLYING COMPANY

A couple years after Hubert Latham's infamous midair duck hunt over the Bolsa Chica Wetlands in 1910, the Japanese community in Wintersburg and Smeltzer decided they, too, would invest in a newfangled flying machine—or, more specifically, an aviator.

Wintersburg Village community in front of Koha Takeishi biplane in Wintersburg, March 1913. *Furuta family collection.*

THE PEATLANDS AVIATOR

Koha Takeishi had become acquainted with some of the peatlands' prominent residents during his breaks from Utah State University. A student from Japan, he worked as a laborer in the celery fields of

Wintersburg and Smeltzer (both present-day Huntington Beach) to make extra money.

In addition to his studies, Takeishi worked at the *Rokki Jiho* (*Rocky Mountain Times*), a Japanese-language newspaper in Utah. He also attended the short-lived Curtiss School of Aviation at North Island, San Diego—a competitor of the Wright Brothers Flying School.

The *Journal of San Diego History* describes the Curtiss training planes, known as "Lizzys" as "composed of bamboo, spruce rods, wire and cloth…deliberately underpowered to prevent flight." Curtiss is reported as joking about the jerry-rigged training plane's quality, saying that "other pupils standing in a group at the end of the field are usually hoping and praying that you will not smash the machine before their turn comes."

After weeks of training on the Lizzy and then a biplane, students graduated after passing an exam that included "five consecutive figure eight's around two pylons set a thousand feet apart, and to make an accurate landing stopping the machine within fifty feet of a given mark." The $500-plus tuition for the aviation class was an expensive proposition for the time; however, Curtiss allowed students to apply the cost to the purchase of an airplane.

J.A.D. McCurdy, aviator in a Curtiss airplane, 1912. *Library of Congress.*

Curtiss's advertisements in national magazines brought more civilian students for the 1911–12 class, described as a "remarkably diverse group of students… including Mohan Singh from India, Motohisa Kondo and Kono [*sic*] Takeishi from Japan, and Captain George Capistini of the Greek army" along with the "Bird Girl, Julia Clark." The inclusion of so many foreign-born students required instructors to sometimes "give the lessons in sign language."

In 1912, Takeishi was the third Japanese civilian pilot to receive his license, becoming a source of community pride for Japanese Americans in the peatlands.

He was in demand as part of the new breed of aviators and part of the Curtiss 1912 advertising campaign, which bragged "seventeen pupils obtained their pilots licenses at our San Diego school." The advertisement did not mention that his classmate "Bird Girl, Julia Clark," had died flying her plane one month after graduating.

The *Ritzville Times* in southeast Washington State gave advance coverage to Takeishi's visit there in October 1912:

> *The business men of Ritzville have made arrangements to have the Japanese aviator who recently made flights to Spokane Interstate Fair come here next week and give a service of three flights. The machine will be brought to Ritzville about Tuesday and assembled, after which it will be placed upon exhibition in a tent. The aviator, Koha Takeishi, will be in the tent most of the time when the machine is not flying and will explain its parts and working to those who desire to learn something about it.*

MEMORIES OF TAKEISHI

Henry Kiyomi Akiyama—the area's most prominent goldfish farmer—talked about Takeishi during his 1982 oral history interview.

"He did not have much money," recalled Akiyama. "So during the celery harvesting time, he came to work at a celery farm and stayed in one of the labor camps. That's how he became acquainted with the other Japanese in Orange County."

Takeishi worked out of Tsuneji Chino's agricultural labor camp. Chino was an educated man and his camp attracted students on break from school. Chino also was associated with the Wintersburg Japanese Presbyterian Mission, and many of his laborers attended the mission on Wintersburg (now Warner) Avenue.

Japanese pilot Sakamoto in Orange County, circa 1916–17. *California State University Fullerton, Center for Oral and Public History, PJA 449.*

Akiyama reported that the college students "lived the same sort of life as other Japanese laborers. But because they were students, they didn't stay long—sometimes one or two weeks, sometimes for a month. And if they got money, they went back to school. As long as they were in the camp, they ate the same food and worked like other Japanese."

Takeishi stood out because of his aviation skills.

Koichi Terahata, a key member of the local Japanese Association, and T.M. Asari, a founding member of the Wintersburg Japanese Presbyterian Mission and goldfish farmer on Wintersburg Avenue, "talked to the Japanese in the county and asked them to buy stock of a new flying company," remembered Akiyama.

"So each one invested $25 in stock payment and a company was formed," explained Akiyama. "Mr. Asari became the president of this company, which was named the Smeltzer Flying Company."

Akiyama explained the Smeltzer Flying Company was not profit motivated: "To have a Japanese pilot was what all the Japanese were proud of and they decided to support...Mr. Takeishi, by forming a company."

Terahata, Asari and other Japanese living in Wintersburg and Smeltzer organized a fundraising organization for Takeishi, raising $4,000 to buy an airplane (an equivalent of well over $90,000 in 2013). The Akiyama oral history includes the notation that Takeishi successfully flew the plane from the Dominguez Field in Los Angeles County to a field in Wintersburg in 1913.

After this, Takeishi's support group of farmers raised more money to send him to the first air show in Japan in 1913, sponsored by *Osaka Asahi* newspaper.

LAST FLIGHT OF THE WHITE DOVE

The *New York Herald*, reporting from Tokyo on May 2, 1913, summarized the day's tragic events: "The Japanese aviator Takeishi, who recently returned from the United States, was killed at Osaka this afternoon. He had a successful flight from Osaka to Kyoto and was on his return. His skull was fractured while he was attempting to alight. Takeishi was well-known in Pacific Coast cities as an aviator."

Takeishi was reported in the *Honolulu Star Bulletin* to have flown to a height of 2,500 feet. The *Ritzville Times* acknowledged the death of "the Japanese aviator who was under contract to make three aeroplane flights in Ritzville last fall."

The November 1913 edition of *Popular Mechanics* described Takeishi's funeral in Japan: "The funeral of Koha Takeishi, the Japanese airman who was killed near the *Fukakusa* Parade Grounds in the Japanese city-to-city flight, was the occasion for an impressive procession in his honor at Osaka recently. The airman had just returned from America and at the time of his fatal accident had nearly accomplished the city-to-city flight in a monoplane named '*Shira-Hato*' or 'White Dove.' His flight attracted nationwide interest in Japan."

The magazine further reported that Takeishi's coffin—adorned with a piece of his plane's broken propeller—was borne by twelve pallbearers and Takeishi's brother, Dr. Joyu Takeishi. Dr. Takeishi is later reported to have sent money from Japan to reimburse the Orange County farmers who had invested in his brother's plane.

Takeishi was the first civilian aviator death for Japan. In 1914, *Popular Mechanics* noted there were more airplane deaths in 1913—192 in total—"than

Koha Takeishi biplane in flight over Wintersburg, 1913. *Furuta family collection.*

in all the years before 1912, since the Wrights made the first public flights in a heavier-than-air machine." Their report included the death of Koha Takeishi.

In 1982, Akiyama shared with his interviewer a photograph he'd kept of Takeishi, taken around 1912 before he left for Japan—a reminder of the once-hopeful Smeltzer Flying Company.

Chapter 11

THE FURUTA FARM AND THE ALIEN LAND LAW

There simply is no easy way to convey the political turmoil that faced Wintersburg's immigrant farmers in the years leading up to 1913. It was painful. The kind of thing we don't talk about much but should. Today, a century later, it is an important civil liberties lesson for future generations.

That Charles Furuta and Reverend Hisakichi Terasawa were able to purchase five acres for the Furuta farm and Wintersburg Japanese

Yukiko Furuta on the front porch of the Furuta home in Wintersburg, 1912–13. *Furuta family collection.*

Presbyterian Mission was a feat of perseverance. That Tsurumatsu Asari was able to purchase land for a farm and goldfish hatchery on Wintersburg Avenue was a small miracle.

In his 1982 oral history interview, Henry Kiyomi Akiyama told his interviewers that these two properties—the Furuta and Asari farms—were the only Japanese-owned properties he knew of prior to the Alien Land Law of 1913.

Purchased in 1908, the Furuta farm and Wintersburg Japanese Presbyterian Mission—one hundred years later—is the only pre–Alien Land Law Japanese-owned property left in urban Orange County.

WEBB-HENEY ACT

California's Webb-Heney Act (Alien Land Law of 1913) prohibited "all aliens ineligible for citizenship" from owning land and prohibited their leasing land for more than three years. Chinese, Japanese, Korean and East Indian immigrant farmers were ineligible for naturalization under U.S. immigration laws. White, African American and Filipino aliens were not affected.

Proponents of the act used early common law as a basis for their complaint—an argument posed in *Sei Fujii v. State of California*—reverting to pre–American Revolution feudalism: "An alien could acquire real property by gift, purchase or devise, but his rights in the property were subject to forfeiture by the crown."

PROTESTS

Assemblyman Bloodgood—a Republican-Progressive from Inglewood—sought an exemption for farm leases. Some accused him of placating big farming and land interests.

U.S. secretary of state William Jennings Bryan traveled to California at the direction of President Woodrow Wilson to tour Japanese farm communities and rural schools. What he saw were successful farm enterprises and close to 100 percent enrollment in schools among the Japanese community. Speaking to the California Legislature in 1913, Bryan urged cooperation between the federal and state government.

William Carter, general secretary of the International Peace Forum, visited Sacramento, urging caution in the interests of world peace. A delegation of landowners from the Island Delta District near Stockton defended the Japanese farm lessees from their region, traveling to Sacramento to voice their protest "against the passage of any alien land ownership bill that would affect the value of property in San Joaquin County."

Dr. Juichi Soyeda—a Japanese attorney delegated by the chambers of commerce of Japan and the Japan America Society to study the Alien Land Law—was asked to speak at the Publishers Association of New York in 1913. As reported by the *New York Times* on June 26, 1913, a representative of the publishers' group said they did not share the opinions of the California legislators and extended "only the most cordial feelings" to the Japanese.

"The thinking men in Japan are well acquainted with the history of the relations between this country and Japan, and of the instances of American fair play which we have experienced," said Soyeda. "The negotiations of the California question are still going on between Washington and Tokio. I cannot but think that the outcome will justify the United States in the light of Christianity and humanity."

The *San Francisco Call* took a stand to counter those who opined that Japanese immigrants posed a social or economic threat, stating it was not based on facts. The *Call* stated there were 158,360 square miles in California, of which the Japanese owned only 20 square miles after a fifty-year presence in California. In a half-page statement on May 1, 1913, the *Call* reasoned,

Tennis on the Furuta farm, Yukiko and Charles Furuta in center, 1913. *Furuta family collection.*

"It will take the Japanese 395,900 years to own California." In the end, these efforts failed, and the Alien Land Law passed.

IN WINTERSBURG

Wintersburg Japanese Presbyterian Mission founder, Cambridge-educated Reverend Hisakichi Terasawa, had encouraged local Japanese to purchase property and put down roots. Charles Furuta and Tsurumatsu Asari—both supporters of the Mission—listened.

Wintersburg landowners, such as the Cole family, worked with local Japanese on a lease or crop-rent basis, including Charles Furuta and Henry Akiyama. The Cole family became so fond of Furuta and Akiyama that they offered them a home on their property and later partnered with Akiyama on his goldfish enterprise.

SEI FUJII V. CALIFORNIA

The Alien Land Laws of 1913 and 1920 remained in place until the Supreme Court of California decided in 1952 that it violated the equal protection clause of the Fourteenth Amendment of the U.S. Constitution. The decision for *Sei Fujii v. California* found that prohibiting land and property ownership to nonwhite immigrants was unconstitutional.

On November 4, 1956, a repeal measure, listed as Proposition 13, was passed by California voters to officially repeal the Alien Land Law, forty-three years after its enactment.

Sei Fujii—a graduate of the University of Southern California law school—was one of the community leaders labeled a subversive element, part of the rationale for Japanese American incarceration during World War II. He is identified in the *Investigation of Un-American Propaganda Activities in the United States*—a report used during congressional hearings in the House of Representatives in 1942—as an adviser to the Central Japanese Association and the North American Branch of the Greater Japan Agricultural Association, as well as being on the boards of several Buddhist Shinto groups. An *Issei*, Fujii was not allowed to become a citizen and was not allowed to practice law in California.

After his World War II incarceration in the Department of Justice Detention Center in Santa Fe, New Mexico, Sei Fujii purchased land in order to challenge the California Alien Land Law with his University of Southern California law school classmate and law partner J. Marion Wright. They succeeded.

Wintersburg Mission congregant Clarence Iwao Nishizu remembered Sei Fujii in his 1982 oral history interview: "I remember distinctly those days when the *Issei* were the discriminatory victims of the Alien Land Laws and Sei Fujii, *Issei* attorney and publisher...used to come to this school [Anaheim Japanese School] to explain to our parents the latest findings of the court cases."

Nishizu told his interviewer, "It may be of interest to you to have me relate what *Issei* were like. They had guts, drive, and were willing to work to get ahead in the face of the discrimination of the Alien Land Law. They wanted to implant a foundation and steppingstone for the *Nisei* to follow."

The *Sei Fujii v. State of California* Supreme Court decision stated:

> *Congress, however, at least prior to 1924, saw fit to permit aliens who are ineligible for citizenship to enter and reside in the United States despite the fact that they could not become naturalized, and such aliens are entitled to the same protection as citizens from arbitrary discrimination.*
>
> *Although Japanese are not singled out by name for discriminatory treatment in the land law, the reference therein to federal standards for*

Furuta family on porch of house in Wintersburg, circa September 1923. *Furuta family collection.*

naturalization which exclude Japanese operates automatically to bring about that result...The California Alien Land Law is obviously designed and administered as an instrument for effectuating racial discrimination, and the most searching examination discloses no circumstances justifying classification on that basis.

There is nothing to indicate that those alien residents who are racially ineligible for citizenship possess characteristics which are dangerous to the legitimate interests of the state, or that they, as a class, might use the land for purposes injurious to public morals, safety or welfare. Accordingly, we hold that the Alien Land Law is invalid as in violation of the Fourteenth Amendment.

Chapter 12

GOLDFISH POND RUMORS

O ne of the rumors reported in an oral history conducted in 1968 with Huntington Beach resident Lee Chamness Jr. relates to Orange County's goldfish farmers.

Chamness was the son of a Huntington Beach city councilman who resigned office to become the town civilian defense coordinator. In this role, he assisted the FBI in arresting Japanese Americans, including those in Wintersburg.

Yukiko Furuta and daughters, circa 1927, near goldfish ponds. *In descending order of height*: Yukiko, Toshiko, Nobuko, Kazuko and Etsuko. *Furuta family collection.*

"During the outbreak of the war [there was] a tremendous goldfish farm with ponds on the ground, and they were all covered with a netting," Chamness—ten-years-old in 1942—told his interviewer. His interview reflected childhood memories of adult conversations, rife with rumors of the time.

"As it happened, all this netting that was covering these ponds were radio antennas," said Chamness. "They had a communication setup with Japan that was unbeatable. They could really talk."

A PROMISING START

Immigrants of western European ancestry in rural Orange County worked with Japanese immigrants on their arrival in the 1890s. Farmers in early 1900s Wintersburg together would face earthquakes, floods, horse thieves, bandits, railroad accidents, influenza and the celery blight. The *Los Angeles Herald* reported in 1910 that Tsurumatsu Asari's poolroom adjoining his market in Wintersburg was robbed at gunpoint of ten dollars, causing Asari to chase the bandits away by firing his own gun five times. It was the pioneer West. Defending one's property and one's neighbors was the code.

When Presbyterian and Methodist Evangelical clergy first walked into the celery fields in 1902 to talk to Japanese laborers, they included Caucasian clergy members from neighboring Westminster. The effort to establish a mission in Wintersburg was supported by both Caucasian and Japanese clergy and by members of various faiths, including those who formed the first Buddhist Church in Orange County, such as Tsurumatsu Asari and an Episcopalian minister, Reverend Hisakichi Terasawa. The mission-building effort received donations from the Japanese around the rural countryside and also from their Caucasian neighbors.

By 1909, the *Los Angeles Herald* reported "two Japanese clergy growers of Smeltzer were elected as directors" of the Celery Growers' Association, joining Caucasian growers on the board. Together, they addressed issues such as "collecting claims from the railroads when the celery had reached the east in poor condition as the result of careless handling." They undoubtedly worked together to address the damaging celery blight affecting crops during that time.

In 1912, Japanese farmers had joined in the effort to rebuild the Huntington Beach pier, destroyed by a Pacific storm. California journalist Neeta Marquis writes in 1913 that "the entire countryside [of Orange County] accepted the invitation of the Japanese to join them in their celebration of the Emperor's last birthday"—the traditional *Tenchsetsu*. It was one of the many diverse cultural events experienced by pioneers, due to the international appeal of Southern California.

The *Huntington Beach News* reported the June 1914 festivities for the rededication of the pier featured an exhibition by Hawaiian Irish surfer George Freeth and a sword dancing and judo demonstration by the Japanese community. Events such as the Armistice and July 4 parades included the Japanese community, the Smeltzer Japanese Association funding the Independence Day's first fireworks display in Huntington Beach beginning in 1905.

The diverse community weathered tragedies that brought its members together. No one escaped the Spanish flu epidemic that swept the country between 1918 and 1919. Nor did they escape the worry and loss of World War I. As Orange County left the second decade of the twentieth century behind, residents gathered to put those tragic events behind them. The *Santa Ana Register* reported in September 1919 that the "Wintersburg folk" honored returning servicemen, including Reverend Junzo Nakamura of the Wintersburg Japanese Presbyterian Mission.

Within days of the Great Kanto Earthquake, which obliterated Yokohama and Tokyo on September 1, 1923, the Huntington Beach City Council took action, authorizing on September 4 "$100 from the Music & Promotion Fund to be paid to the Chamber of Commerce to be used in the Japanese Relief Fund." It was a gesture reflecting the fact that the Japanese were part of the community.

By 1925, chili peppers had overtaken celery as the major crop. Masami Sasaki moved to Huntington Beach and—with a one-thousand-acre operation and ten other growers—formed a chili pepper–processing cooperative on Beach Boulevard. Sasaki and fellow Orange County farmer Shosuke Nitta served on the Orange County Farm Bureau board of directors, with which there was a good relationship. Masakazu Iwata, who recorded voluminous details about the *Issei* farmers in his study *Planted in Good Soil*, specifically remarks the *Issei* were "highly laudatory of the Orange County Farm Bureau," which had worked closely with Japanese farmers on labor issues and farming techniques.

In the mid-1930s—while life in farm country continued—the succession of alien land laws, labor unions agitating against Asian immigration and the associated anti-immigrant rhetoric was having an effect. The San Francisco–

Veteran's Day parade in Huntington Beach, 1928. *California State University Fullerton, Center for Oral and Public History, PJA 056.*

based Asiatic Exclusion League—formed in 1905 by close to seventy labor unions—perpetuated stereotypes and fears. Attorney and journalist Carey McWilliams—in a 1935 essay in the *Nation*—blasts California politicians, writing that the anti-Japanese propaganda in the state "has always been characterized by its offensive stupidity."

Later, in 1944, McWilliams—a graduate of the University of Southern California law school—observes that the country failed to recognize California was part of the emerging Pacific Rim and failure to address the prejudices in California led to failed foreign policy. He also examines the disconnect between individual Californian's personal experience and the group mentality, writing "paradoxically, the Japanese were warmly regarded in California, on an individual-to-individual basis, but personal friendship for a particular Japanese seldom changed the attitude toward the group as a whole. Leaders of the anti-Oriental agitation in California will tell you that 'some of my best friends' are Japanese."

McWilliams quotes sociologist Dr. Robert E. Park, explaining that "public opinion is the public mind in unstable equilibrium."

The growing anti-Japanese pressure was more prominent in the cities—where land use covenants restricted where people of color lived—and in the politics of northern California, San Francisco and the state's capital. McWilliams notes, "The southern part of the state and the rural areas generally were not favorable to the agitation."

In integrated northwest Orange County, the *Nisei*—the generation born in America—attended the Ocean View Grammar School in Wintersburg and, later, Huntington Beach High School. They were part of football and track teams, played on the beach at Huntington Beach and listened to the same music on the radio, and their names were recorded in the high school's yearbooks. Orange County was the only home they had known.

DELIVERING VEGETABLES

Clarence Nishizu was going about his regular routine on December 7, 1941, delivering vegetables to the city market in Los Angeles when he was stopped by the police.

"The officer, with pistol in hand, excoriated me with profane language and all but said that I started the war. I was really scared," recalled Nishizu in his 1982 interview. "Other *Nisei* shared my fear and accompanying depression. The general public viewed us with suspicion as if we had committed something wrong. Even the attitude of our next door Caucasian neighbor suddenly changed. We were disheartened as to our future. We were in a quandary."

IN TALBERT

James Kanno—who became the first Japanese American mayor of a continental U.S. city—was interviewed in 1971. He was fifteen at the time of Pearl Harbor, working with his father, Shuji, on the family farm in Talbert (present-day Fountain Valley). Shuji was an elder in the Wintersburg Japanese Presbyterian Church and a teacher at a Japanese Language School in Costa Mesa, supported by the church.

"I was out in the field with my dad helping him irrigate. We were just setting the pipes out there on the field to irrigate, and then our neighbor came over and said, 'Pearl Harbor has been bombed! We're at war with Japan,'" recalled Kanno. "So my dad said, 'Gee, we'd better go to the house and listen to the radio and hear what's happening.' And he said, 'Well, I was afraid this might happen.' So we rushed to the house and glued our ears to the radio."

Attending Santa Ana High School at the time, James remembered the school's principal called an assembly and told the students that "the Japanese Americans coming to this high school are not Japanese, but they are Americans; that the rest of the students shouldn't look down upon the Japanese American students coming to our school; that we're all from different backgrounds; and that this is typical of America...I thought it was very nice. It sort of helped us out, I'm sure."

He later recalls the discussion in his civics class about potential evacuation of Japanese from the West Coast, telling them, "This is America. This is a democratic country, and I'm a citizen, so it's impossible. I can't be evacuated. I remember this precise statement."

ON THE FURUTA FARM

Yukiko Furuta was home recovering from surgery when Pearl Harbor happened. Her children were away at the engagement party of her niece Sumi Akiyama to John Aiso, who would become a prominent California attorney and judge and head instructor of the Military Intelligence Service Language School (MIS). Yukiko's husband, Charles, was working in the fields. Reverend Sohei Kowta was living next door in the manse with his family at the Wintersburg Japanese Presbyterian Church, on the northwest corner of the Furuta farm. He walked over to tell Yukiko what happened.

In her 1982 oral history interview, she recalled being shocked, thinking "there had been a war between Japan and China...that was enough."

Her interpreter explained in 1982, "She thought her children were Americans, so she thought her children would be drafted and they'd have to fight against Japan...she thought she herself would have to die because that was the rule of samurai families. But she worried little about that because she had only one son and the rest were daughters. So they wouldn't have to send all their children to the war."

Charles Furuta was president of the Smeltzer Japanese Association that year. Yukiko recalled that he was "was expecting the FBI to take him, because he was a leader of the community...he had already packed a suitcase with warm clothing, and was ready."

AT WINTERSBURG JAPANESE PRESBYTERIAN CHURCH

Tadashi Kowta, son of Reverend Sohei Kowta, hid by the chicken coop behind the manse in Wintersburg when the FBI came to question his father. Only eleven years old at the time, Kowta wondered "what was going to happen to me, our family—Japan and the U.S. were at war, my mother was frail. I wondered whether I had to take responsibility for the family, if they did something to my father."

"ALL CONVERSATION STOPPED"

An anonymous oral history, conducted in 1966 and held in the archives at the Center for Oral and Public History at California State University–Fullerton, describes the change in community attitude.

"Well, naturally, they were all suspicious of us, because everything in the paper was about war and was anti-Japanese…as soon as they saw us, they would say, 'There goes a damn Jap!'" explains the interviewee, who eventually was evacuated in 1942 along with other Orange County Japanese

Clamming at Huntington Beach, 1935. *California State University Fullerton, Center for Oral and Public History, PJA 355.*

Americans from the Huntington Beach Pacific Electric Railway station. "That's the feeling I got, that any time you went anyplace, all conversation stopped, and there was just a cold feeling, like we were escaped prisoners."

THE TEACHERS

Aiko Tanamachi Endo remembered Huntington Beach High School during her 1983 interview.

"I participated in and lettered in every sport, including basketball, baseball, and hockey. I had swimming in gym…I played on the tennis team," recalled Endo. One of her teachers wanted to personally intervene and stop her evacuation.

"I can remember when we found out that we had to evacuate, how our Latin and algebra teacher, Miss Margaret Bliss—she was a dear soul—just thought it was terrible that we had to evacuate. So she said, 'I'm going to find out if I can keep you girls with me,'" Endo recalled.

"She was a dear," remembered Endo, about Miss Bliss trying to help her and her friend Toyoko Kitajima. "We realized there was just no way. I told her I was sure that there was no way she could keep us."

Bliss, who had begun teaching at the high school in 1927, was among the Huntington Beach High School teachers and administrators who helped students continue their studies and graduate after evacuation. Vice-principal Ray Elliott maintained correspondence with Wintersburg goldfish farmer Harley Asari, a former student, and was a link to home while Asari was confined at the Colorado River Relocation Center at Poston, Arizona.

"NONE OF US WANTED TO GO"

"Naturally, none of us wanted to go. It was our home. We were born and raised here," explained Henry Kanegae during his 1966 oral history interview. Kanegae also was evacuated from Huntington Beach in May 1942. He did not recall widespread discrimination in Orange County after Pearl Harbor, except for "small, isolated cases where some individual was abusive and so forth, but nothing real noticeable or unusual."

The *Issei* generation was more outwardly accepting of the circumstances as *shikata ga nai*, or something that "cannot be helped," while more of the *Nisei* had questions.

"We felt there was really no reason for us to be forced to go," said Kanegae, "except for the fact that the government felt that we should."

THE DAYS THAT FOLLOWED

About ten at the time, Lee Chamness Jr. recalled in his 1966 interview why the FBI approached his father—then a Huntington Beach city councilman—for assistance after Pearl Harbor. His oral history is punctuated with laughter, noted by his interviewer.

"Well, the F.B.I. contacted him because he was in the produce business in this area. He had a trucking business and then he had a couple of markets here, so he bought a lot of things from the Japanese farmers out here. Most all of the Japanese in this area were farmers; in fact, all of them that I can remember were. He knew them all very personally—I mean, business-wise," Chamness told his interviewer. "And the men went out, I think, that night and then the women the next day or so. They gave the women time to pack and so forth. They were dangerous, I guess [laughter]."

Chamness recalls his father—who owned a market off Main Street in Huntington Beach—being armed with a .38 pistol and believes the FBI agents also were armed. The guns were not needed.

"As far as I ever heard him tell, they never went in using a show of force, because it wasn't necessary," said Chamness. "That's why the F.B.I. had him along, because he knew all these people, he knew them by their first names. He went, more or less, to explain to them what was going to happen and that they were just trying to use preventive measures…there very well could have been a lot of action taken against people that were good American citizens."

Chamness's interview is a mix of positive comments about the Japanese community and a repeat of many of the rumors he heard as a child, such as radio netting across goldfish ponds, plots by the Black Dragon Society, a house with a dynamite cache and a chili pepper farmer who had "pumps they could hook to a fire hydrant—close to our water reservoir—and they could pump poison back in the line clear to the reservoir [laughter]. That would have been catastrophic. Poison the whole water system."

The Akiyama family in Wintersburg, 1927. *California State University Fullerton, Center for Oral and Public History, PJA 521.*

When questioned about the specifics, Chamness states he does not know any but remembers his father talking about it.

The army set up a command post off Main Street in Huntington Beach, in Lake Park. Military ships anchored offshore near the pier. A gunnery was installed in the Bolsa Chica Wetlands. Huntington Beach grammar school students practiced evacuating into the bomb shelter. Everyone learned how to put out incendiary fires with sand.

In the seventh grade near the end of the war, Chamness was put to work as a runner between the command posts in town.

"We had a steel hat, an arm band, and a gas mask. And we would run from station to station delivering messages…they didn't have any men to take the job. There was nobody here, since everybody had gone to the service," explained Chamness. "Everybody did something—everybody. There were men, women and kids all together doing something. My mother was one of the spotters on top of our tallest building in town, the Memorial Hall."

Orange County judo competition on September 12, 1930. *California State University Fullerton, Center for Oral and Public History, PJA 260.*

One of those first taken by the FBI, according to federal teletypes issuing warrants for the arrests of California Japanese, was Kamenosuke Aoki, a chili pepper grower who was part of Masami Sasaki's large chili pepper cooperative in Huntington Beach.

Kamenosuke and his son, Iwao, had purchased a wooden building from the Standard Oil Company and moved it to a fifteen-acre property with chili dehydrators on the east side of Beach Boulevard, between Garfield Avenue and Adams Street. The Aoki kendo or judo hall became the center of judo clubs around the county, hosting competitions. The hall also was used in 1935 to host the Southern California Buddhist convention.

Aoki was the chili pepper farmer mentioned in the oral history of Lee Chamness Jr. in 1968 as "this fellow that had the pepper farm.

"He was supposedly one of the top men in the Black Dragon Society," said Chamness. "They were to develop, had they been given time, an underground movement in this area."

Clarence Nishizu described in 1983 what happened to Aoki after Pearl Harbor.

"Mr. Aoki, being deeply involved in kendo, was accused of being head of the Black Dragon Society," explained Nishizu (whose own father, Shinjiro, was picked up by the FBI on December 12). "All of the kendo equipment was confiscated...kendo alluded to the militarism of Japan and had a bad public image."

Chili pepper drying at Bolsa, 1925. *California State University Fullerton, Center for Oral and Public History, PJA 052.*

Tetsuden Kashima writes in *Judgment Without Trial: Japanese American Imprisonment During World War II* in 2011, about a file kept on the Black Dragon Society in the Central Records Facility in the U.S. Army intelligence branch Counter Intelligence Corps. The file was examined by Henry Miyatake in 1953, then a Counter Intelligence Corps special agent working at the Central Records Facility in Maryland.

The Southern California version of the Black Dragon Society sounds more like a men's club common to the time period. Kashima explains Miyatake found that "the records show that a group of Los Angeles *Kibei* created the [Black Dragon Society] as a way to cover their repeated absences from their wives and homes. Their activities were confined to drinking, gambling and carousing…When Agent Miyatake talked with other CIC agents, one officer told him that the subversive nature of this organization was a government creation."

BY ORDER OF THE PRESIDENT

The list of arrests from the "custodial detention" files of the FBI include Wintersburg goldfish farmer Tsurumatsu Asari, the "chili pepper king" Masami Sasaki and Talbert farmer Gensuke Masuda, a congregant of the Wintersburg Japanese Presbyterian Church whose son, Kazuo Masuda, was already enlisted in the U.S. Army and who eventually would have four sons serving in the U.S. military. The files include handwritten notations noting the date each person was apprehended.

The December 7, 1941 warrant from the Office of Attorney General to the director of the FBI in Washington, D.C., authorizes agents "to arrest or cause the arrest of each of the following alien enemies…whom I deem dangerous to the public peace and safety of the United States" and instructs agents that "each of such persons is to be detained and confined until further order. By order of the President."

FBI teletypes indicate that by December 8—within twenty-four hours of Pearl Harbor—310 Japanese had been detained by the Los Angeles bureau, including Japanese in Orange County. The teletypes note that the FBI had begun looking for residents with "German tendencies." By December 10, a memorandum from the FBI in Los Angeles to Washington, D.C., about events in the Los Angeles area reports that it has "a large squad of men at the Immigration place, has 9 men in the office for complaints and telephone calls and a large number of men at the various precincts yet because they are still bringing in stragglers."

Another December 10 memorandum from J. Edgar Hoover to Major General Edwin M. Watson provides a map of the United States showing the locations where Japanese "aliens" were taken into custody, the largest number by far in Southern California.

The strain was beginning to show. Interoffice memorandums in the FBI reveal a squabble about communications, the special agent in charge writing "only half of the persons who should be picked up have to date been apprehended because we have not gone into the citizens group; and it is [Curtis Munson's, a special representative of the State Department] impression from what he has learned here on the Coast that the citizens who are disloyal constitute a large group of possible troublemakers in the emergency. He feels that the apprehension of the aliens is only half of the job, and the citizens constitute the other half of it."

The Franklin D. Roosevelt Presidential Library and Museum collection contains a memorandum from the assistant to Attorney General James

H. Rowe Jr. to President Roosevelt's private secretary, Grace Tully, several months after the initial arrests. Rowe, a critic of the proposal to relocate and confine Japanese Americans, denounced the proposal as unconstitutional and a result of public hysteria.

"Please tell the President to keep an eye on the Japanese situation in California," writes Rowe on February 2, 1942. "It looks to me like it will explode any day now…There are about 125,000 of them, and if it happens, it will be one of the great mass exoduses of history. It would probably require suspension of the writ of habeas corpus—and my estimate of the country's present feeling is that we would have another Supreme Court fight on our hands."

Rowe's communication is followed by a memorandum from Attorney General Francis Biddle directly to President Roosevelt on February 17, 1942. Biddle criticized the media that was fueling anti–Japanese American sentiment.

"It is extremely dangerous for the columnists, acting as 'Armchair Strategists and Junior G-Men,' to suggest that an attack on the West Coast and planned sabotage is imminent when the military authorities and the F.B.I. have indicated that this is not the fact," writes Biddle, three days before President Roosevelt signed Executive Order 9066, which authorized forced evacuation. "It comes close to shouting FIRE! in the theater; and if race riots occur these writers will bear a heavy responsibility…it would serve to clarify the situation in the public mind if you see fit to mention it."

UN-AMERICAN ACTIVITIES

Eight days after President Roosevelt signed Executive Order 9066, a report called the *Investigation of Un-American Propaganda Activities in the United States* was published and was used during congressional hearings in the House of Representatives. It claimed that the proximity of farmers near oil facilities in California was justification for evacuation. One section refers to the "Japanese problem in California."

"Prior to the Japanese attack on Pearl Harbor, extreme carelessness marked the policy of the United States with reference to the location of Japanese residents of California," notes the February 28, 1942 report, which included photographs of farms near oil tanks in southern California. "These potential saboteurs were permitted to take up residence or to carry on their business and their truck gardening in the immediate vicinity of important defense establishments, oil storage tanks, oil wells, harbors, and the like."

The report fails to mention that the vast majority of farmers in areas like Huntington Beach—regardless of their ethnicity—worked among the oil fields that covered the land. It congratulates the federal government for taking "steps to cope with the menace...by giving the Army authority to move the Japanese population from those areas where they have been in a position to do incalculable sabotage."

Using records from Japanese organizations that had sent aid to Japan during its prior conflict in China, the *Investigation of Un-American Propaganda Activities* in the United States tallies amounts donated for "crisis bundles," including a $20.00 contribution from the "Talbot" Language School (the Talbert Language School), and approximately $425.00 from the Costa Mesa Produce and Japanese Language School. Both language schools were supported by the Wintersburg Japanese Presbyterian Church, the land for the Costa Mesa school having been donated by Southern California heiress Fanny Bixby Spencer in 1930 (outcast from society as a feminist and socialist).

The same congressional report also details the individuals associated with the Japanese associations, providing lists of names. For the Smeltzer association, Charles Furuta is listed by his Japanese name, Mitsuji Furuta, as president, along with vice-president Hichiro Nagamutsu, treasurers Satomi Tsuchimi and Shuji Kanno (the father of Fountain Valley's first mayor, James Kanno, and an elder in the Wintersburg Japanese Presbyterian Church) and secretary Hikichi Iwamoto. The report mangles the name of the association, referring to it as the "Smelsa" Japanese Association and lists the associations' suspect activities as including the collection of tin foil.

Much of the report is McCarthyesque and more revealing of the lack of understanding of Japanese American culture. Decades later, Congressional hearings in the 1980s determined no person of Japanese ancestry, *Issei* or *Nisei*, had committed an act against the United States. The facts revealed during the decades that followed led to the Civil Liberties Act of 1988 and redress.

THEY WERE GONE

By early 1942, the entire Japanese community of Orange County—and that of the West Coast—was placed in the category of a potential national

Mary Chino with unknown, Tsuneji Chino, Toyo Chino, Tom Terahata and Sumi Akiyama at Huntington Beach, 1917. *California State University Fullerton, Center for Oral and Public History, PJA 522.*

security threat and plans were made to evacuate them to confinement centers. Lives created over the prior four decades were falling apart.

Lee Chamness Jr. was asked by his oral history interviewer whether there was "anybody in the community that was really adamant about getting rid of the Japanese Americans, all of them, right away?"

"Not that I know of. I never heard it mentioned. I never heard anything about getting rid of the Japanese. All I can recall is things happening," recalled Chamness in 1966. "Of course, they were happening very fast; our Civil Defense had to be organized and the Army was moving in to the beach...but all the Japanese population in this area was gone. Like I said, right after the war broke out they were gone. The very next day there were no kids in school from the Japanese families...they were gone."

Chapter 13

THE SUNDAY BEFORE

Those not acquainted with the West Coast conditions in the spring of 1942 could hardly grasp the significance and faith revealed in these messages.
The Sunday Before, *May 1945*

Theologian E. Stanley Jones wrote a forward to a little-known mimeographed collection of sermons by West Coast Japanese American clergymen delivered in the days before evacuation and confinement, *The Sunday Before.* Jones—himself a Methodist missionary who was nominated for the Nobel Peace Prize and a recipient of the Gandhi Peace Award—observed in 1945 that he saw "a spirit meeting disaster in a triumphant way and making it into something else."

Among the sermons recorded is one by the Reverend Sohei Kowta, clergyman at the

Reverend Sohei Kowta with George, Ann and nineteenth-month-old Robbie Jeane Yanase at the Evergreen Hostel in Los Angeles after incarceration at the Colorado River Relocation Center, June 1945. *Charles E. Mace, University of California Berkeley, Bancroft Library, WRA no. H-702.*

Wintersburg Japanese Presbyterian Church from 1938 until evacuation in 1942. Reverend Kowta and his family lived in the 1910 manse next to the mission building.

REVEREND SOHEI KOWTA

The Sunday Before includes a preface to the sermons, describing each pastor who wrote it. Reverend Kowta's description was written about his time in Wintersburg.

"Young people used to come to Rev. Kowta's church from miles around," explains the pamphlet, describing how Wintersburg Village functioned as the heart of Orange County's Japanese community:

> *He has no gray hairs; he wears a short stubby moustache; his eyes are sharp, but ever have an infectious smile of both eyes and mouth. His good-natured banter lightens up the sometimes too solemn meetings of the church federation.*
>
> *He is probably one of the best English speakers amongst Issei preachers. At the same time, he puts his main point over in the old style; it is suggested rather than hammered home; it is left in the background to be sensed by the imagination rather than to be analyzed with words.*

THE KOWTA FAMILY

Reverend Kowta's children have memories of living at the manse in Wintersburg Village.

"I remember the very high ceiling in the bedroom [of the manse], which seemed like a social hall," recalls Tadashi Kowta, the eldest of the Kowta children. "When I visited the manse about 10 to 15 years later, I bumped my head on the ceiling of one of the back rooms."

"The Church was painted white and it stood out in the neighborhood, since there were no high rise buildings. The area was flat with farmlands," remembers Tadashi Kowta. At the time, the Furuta children were adults in their twenties and other children to play with were scattered throughout the farmlands. Tadashi Kowta particularly recalled the Akiyama, Furuta, Kanegae, Kanno and Nitta families.

Riyo Kowta and children with their car in front of the Wintersburg Japanese Presbyterian manse, circa 1938. *Kowta family collection.*

"The Church had a large backyard," Tadashi Kowta relays. "So we raised animals, such as sheep, mallard ducks, chicken, etc. Next door neighbors were the Furutas with their gold fish farm, which we visited periodically."

"Near the manse, there was a grocery store," remembers Tadashi Kowta, referring to the Tashima Market (formerly the Asari Market). "I had gone there to purchase something and I was in the checkout line. A policeman in his uniform came up to me and grabbed me. I was so scared and I don't remember what he said. He let go of me and told me he was only kidding."

Tadashi Kowta remembers "a slaughterhouse very close to the church." This would have been the butcher referred to by Yukiko Furuta in her 1984 oral history as MacIntosh's "meat house" on what is now Nichols Lane. J.W. McIntosh—the McIntosh Market Company—and his large family were another of Wintersburg's early pioneer families, having arrived in the nineteenth century from Nova Scotia and grazed cattle on the Bolsa Chica pastureland near Wintersburg. Their beef market later was acquired by the Alpha Beta chain.

Tadashi said he "faintly" remembers the church services, "which I attended faithfully," and described a favorite Christmas morning at the manse.

"One Christmas, probably when I was 9 or 10, I received a baseball glove from my parents," Tadashi Kowta recalls. "It was one of my joyous moments and I climbed onto their bed while they were still in it and pounded the glove with glee." He remembers taking the glove to the Ocean View Grammar School to play softball.

The Kowtas visited Japan before moving to their new ministry assignment in Wintersburg, where the Kowta children were enrolled at the Ocean View Grammar School. Tadashi Kowta explains his mother's health was fragile. The family lived with his grandparents for two years so his mother, Riyo, could receive help raising Tadashi, his brother, Makoto, and sister, Hiroko.

"When we came back from Japan, I was placed in the first grade at age 8 years," writes Tadashi Kowta, who says his favorite class was mathematics. "I have jokingly stated that I was the dumbest kid on the block for I was in the first grade for the third time! I attended the first two grades in San Francisco, where I was born, then to Tokyo and Shizuoka for two years. I was placed in the first grade, since I did not know Japanese. Then to Ocean View's first grade, since I did not know English. I soon moved up to the third grade."

Tadashi Kowta also attended the Costa Mesa Japanese Language School associated with the Wintersburg Japanese Presbyterian Church, where his father, Reverend Kowta, also fulfilled the role of superintendent.

DECEMBER 1941

"On December 7th or 8th, the F.B.I. came to interrogate my father, since he was the pastor, superintendent of the Japanese Language School, and probably by inference, a leader of the Japanese community," remembers Tadashi Kowta. Reverend Kowta is remembered as quietly summoning the strength necessary to support his family and his congregants.

"I did not know who he was," says Tadashi Kowta of the FBI agent, describing that day at the manse, "but the door to my father's study room was closed for what I thought was several days. In reading my father's diary after his death, I learned that it was only a day."

"Nevertheless, during that time, I remember sitting by the chicken coop tearfully wondering what was going to happen to me, our family—Japan and the U.S. were at war, my mother was frail," Tadashi Kowta recalls the worry. "I wondered whether I had to take responsibility for the family, if they did something to my father, questioning whether I could assume that kind of responsibility for I was only 11 years old!"

"In May 1942, we left Ocean View Grammar School," Tadashi Kowta describes their mandatory evacuation on May 15, 1942, for an unknown future in confinement. Teachers and children came to say goodbye.

"The whole school seemed to have come to say, 'good bye' to us," says Tadashi Kowta, of Ocean View Grammar School, reminiscent of others' oral histories about Huntington Beach High School at the time of evacuation. "Even though I did not know where we were going, it felt nice to receive a sendoff."

THE SUNDAY BEFORE

For one of his last sermons before internment, Reverend Kowta traveled to the Japanese Union Church in Little Tokyo, for the installation of Reverend Donald Toriumi. His message—memorialized in the booklet *The Sunday Before*—is likely one he delivered to his congregants in Wintersburg.

Reverend Kowta raises the imagery of Abraham and the mass migration of a people into the desert. His message recognizes the hardship and uncertainty in the days ahead and reminds his congregants that "Abraham went out not knowing whither he went," asking them to have faith.

"Ever since the problem of evacuation became public," expands Reverend Kowta, "the Japanese people have been very inquisitive about it. 'Where does the government want us to go? When does the government want us to move? How does the government move us there? How will the government treat us there?'"

Reverend Kowta invoked the lessons of hope and self-sacrificing love, telling his congregants to prepare themselves spiritually as well as materially for evacuation, and that "every crisis is a testing time of one's character." Reverend Kowta continued:

> *Fully equipped with these virtues, we shall have nothing to be afraid of. Give us a desert; we shall make it a beautiful garden; give us a wasted land, we shall change it into a productive field; give us a wilderness, we shall convert it into a fruitful orchard. Provide for our children competent teachers; regardless of the buildings we shall have, we shall make ours one of the finest schools in the country.*

Colorado River Relocation Center at Poston, Arizona, 1944. *California State University Fullerton, Center for Oral and Public History, PJA 434.*

In this critical hour, the spiritual anguish of the Japanese people is undescribable [sic], their mental perplexity unsoluable [sic], their economic loss inestimable. The mighty economic structure which the Issei have constructed with their sweat and blood during these past several decades is fast crumbling down to its foundation. We shall not foolishly look back, and weep and mourn, and turn ourselves into pillars of salt...but, with faith, hope and love, we shall go wherever God wants us to go.

POSTON

"I remember the dust storms and the deep dry powdery dirt in which our feet sank when we walked," recalls Tadashi Kowta of the Colorado River Relocation Center. He covered up the knot holes that let wind and sand into their barrack with the ends of tin cans.

He remembers his father obtaining a large tank in which to grow carp, providing the blood to his mother, Riyo, as a means of strengthening her health. The majority of those at Poston and other confinement camps began producing food as soon as they were able, to supplement the poor food provided by the government.

Tadashi Kowta participated "in the youth worship services and attending the adult services, I believe, in the auditorium. We watched the movies outdoor and we took a charcoal heater to keep us warm. I was in the Boy Scouts and was the flag bearer, since I was the only one with a full uniform. I swam backstroke in the 'canal' and placed in the swim meet."

Reverend Kowta, who had attended a theological seminary in Dayton, Ohio, began to help organize the various denominations of clergy into interfaith support for the displaced community, serving on Poston's interfaith council. *The Sunday Before* publication notes remarkably positive correspondence from Reverend Kowta about his work in the trying circumstances of confinement: "From the camp he writes: 'It is a real joy for me to be on the job day and night. Very fortunately, the American officials are very thoughtful and understanding. We get along splendidly.'"

In turn, the federal government's November 1945 *Final Report for the Colorado River Relocation Center Community Activities Section* notes, "The maintaining of a united church was made possible by a very tactful moderator, Reverend Sohei Kowta, of the Presbyterian Church."

THE RETURN

By 1945, the Kowtas left Poston and returned to the Little Tokyo district in Los Angeles, to assist at the Japanese Union Church. Once again, Reverend Kowta was a leader in an interfaith and multicultural outreach effort in what had become Bronzeville. The history website www.bronzeville-la.com summarizes the events leading to this move:

> *Bronzeville in downtown Los Angeles existed for about three short years in the 1940s. The area known as Little Tokyo transformed into the African American enclave of Bronzeville during World War II after Japanese Americans were evicted from their West Coast homes and placed into United States confinement camps.*
>
> *As World War II progressed, Los Angeles faced a labor shortage in the war industries, and a huge migration of African Americans, mainly from the Deep South, started to flood the Southland to seek employment. Thousands ended up in the vacant Little Tokyo buildings because most of*

Los Angeles had restrictive housing covenants that barred people of color from living in white neighborhoods.

During the war years, the Pilgrim House for the African American migrant community set up space in the Japanese Union Church building, which also housed belongings of the Japanese Americans in confinement. In 1945, as Japanese Americans began to return, the Pilgrim House established the Common Ground Committee "to help promote a favorable atmosphere for returning Japanese Americans and to foster positive racial interaction among the African Americans, Japanese Americans and Latino Americans in the area."

The Pilgrim House and the Japanese Union Church began sharing space. Reverend Sohei Kowta worked to bring people in trying circumstances together, serving on the Pilgrim House board. During the following years through 1950, the Pilgrim House eventually returned the space to the Japanese Union Church.

The National Park Service (NPS) notes Reverend Kowta's efforts to help Japanese Americans returning from confinement in *Five Views: An Ethnic Historic Site Survey for California*: "Rev. Sohei Kowta…recognized the need to establish a center to aid Japanese Americans returning from the concentration camps. Along with the Presbytery and the American Friends Service Committee, he established a resettlement center…known as the Evergreen Hostel, and Rev. Kowta conducted religious services for Union Church members and other residents."

Reverend Kowta and Esther Rhoades managed the hostel, which received no funding from the War Relocation Authority. It was located at 506 North Evergreen Street in Los Angeles's Boyle Heights district and had operated as Presbyterian school for Japanese children prior to the war. The Evergreen Hostel building—constructed in 1914—remains standing a century later as the Fellowship House.

A couple blocks from the Evergreen Hostel is the historic Evergreen Cemetery, which includes a "Garden of the Pines" section with a 1966 memorial to the *Issei* and the graves of Japanese American Medal of Honor recipients. Also buried there are notable figures such as photographer Toyo Miyatake, who photographed Japanese Americans in confinement during World War II, and a monument to the wealthy Bixby family. (Fanny Bixby Spencer donated land to Japanese Americans in Costa Mesa, Orange County, California, which supported one of the Wintersburg Japanese Presbyterian Church's language schools, and adopted two Japanese American children.)

The Evergreen Cemetery also was home to the 1877-era nine-acre "potter's field" where indigent Angelenos were buried beginning in the nineteenth century. Uncovered in 2005, a mass transit project revealed the remains of 174 bodies, Chinese immigrants who had been banned from burial at other cemeteries, their gravestones removed and forgotten. The nearby Evergreen Hostel was located in an area that historically had been home to Los Angeles diverse pioneer population.

It was common for multiple families to share a room at the hostel when they first returned from confinement. Both housing and jobs were scarce for everyone in Southern California after the war. The University of California–Berkeley's Bancroft Collection describes the hostel offering three meals a day and dormitory accommodations "provided at only $1 per person per day for the first week, and $1.50 from then on. The meals are prepared in a clean kitchen by fellow guests, who all partake of the housekeeping duties in the operation of the hostel. The Evergreen Hostel cares for 80 to 90 guests at one time." The Evergreen Hostel was a resting place for those who had lost their homes and farms during the war but had returned to California to start again.

Tadashi Kowta thrived after the return to California. He attended Roosevelt High School in Los Angeles, participating in sports, was elected class officer and maintained perfect attendance. From there, he attended Occidental College, Los Angeles City College and California State University–Los Angeles. By 1953, he was drafted into the U.S. Army and served in military intelligence in Japan. On his return, he graduated from the School of Social Work at the University of Southern California and began working for the Veterans Administration. He was ordained an elder in 1962, the year before his father's passing.

Reverend Kowta continued his work and association with the Union Church in Los Angeles until his passing in 1963, helping his congregants rebuild their lives. His words "on the eve of the greatest mass migration this country has ever witnessed" are those of someone recognizing he could not stop the evacuation and instead choosing to focus his energy on helping others endure it. He reminds in his sermon before evacuation that during a time of crisis "generous people reveal their generosity to a great[er] degree than they do at other times."

As of the beginning of 2014, the children of Reverend Sohei Kowta and Riyo Kowta—Tadashi, Hiroko and Makoto—remain in California.

Chapter 14

THE TASHIMAS
OF WINTERSBURG

Pat Tashima: "Does anything stand out in your mind about Wintersburg?"
*Masako Tashima: "I feel so nice, happy. And people in my neighborhood so nice
to me and my family. So glad."*

When Pat Tashima interviewed her grandmother Masako Yagi Tashima thirty-eight years ago in 1974 for the California State University–Fullerton Japanese American Project, Masako was seventy-eight years old. She was the oldest *Nisei* (first-generation American) in Orange County at the time.

The Masunaga-Takayama store in Stanton, Orange County, California, circa 1925, similar to the Tashima Market in Wintersburg. *California State University Fullerton, Center for Oral and Public History, PJA 237.*

Masako's parents had emigrated from Japan in the late 1800s. They established a hotel in San Francisco, where Masako was born in 1896. Like many other Japanese, her parents had been affected by the post-Meiji period dismantling of the samurai in Japanese society.

The National Park Service report on the *History of Japanese Americans in California: Patterns of Settlement and Occupational Characteristics* states that in 1890, 590 Japanese were in San Francisco. Masako's parents were among them.

"My parents both come from *Samurai* family, and not very much," remembered Masako, "So they were thinking, 'Come outside, see foreign country.'" Her father and mother were nineteen and seventeen years old, respectively, when they left Japan for a new life.

Masako's parents sent her to Japan for school during her younger years, bringing her back for their move to Los Angeles. The NPS reports many Japanese moved from northern to Southern California during the rapid expansion of the Los Angeles area (the early twentieth-century Southern California boom period) and that many moved south in 1906 after the San Francisco earthquake.

In Los Angeles, Masako met her husband, Gunjiro, and they moved to Wintersburg Village.

THE TASHIMA MARKET IN WINTERSBURG

The Tashima Market in Wintersburg was the former Asari Market, owned by Tsurumatsu "T.M." Asari. Gunjiro had been a delivery boy for Asari, before taking ownership of the market himself.

Yukiko Furuta described in her oral history that the store—which specialized in Japanese groceries and clothing—was fairly large, including a barbershop and pool hall. The market was located across the street from the Wintersburg Japanese Presbyterian Mission and the Furuta family home on Wintersburg Avenue.

"All Japanese people who lived around here bought their groceries from this store," explained Yukiko, who was able to walk across Wintersburg Avenue to the market. "The people lived scattered and not too close to the store...So, the store hired delivery boys." Yukiko recalled Wintersburg residents also shopped at MacIntosh's Meat House, off what is now Nichols Lane, and that the Tashima and MacIntosh Markets were the only ones in Wintersburg.

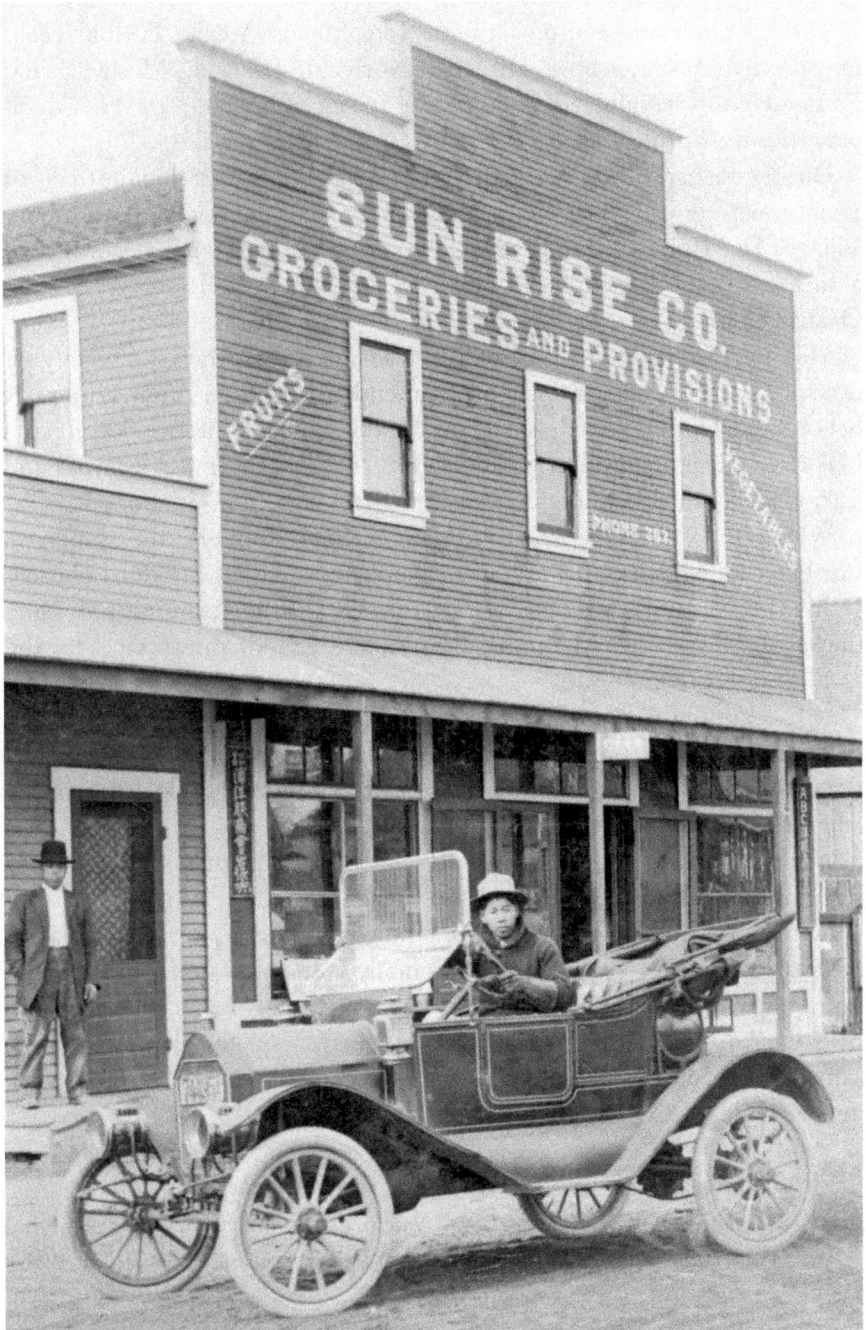

Sun Rise Co. market at Talbert Avenue and Bushard Street, 1910. Yasumatsu Miyawaki standing. *California State University Fullerton, Center for Oral and Public History, PJA 031.*

The Tashima and Furuta families were friends. Yukiko Furuta recalls that the five Tashima boys (Hiroyuki, Noriyuki, Takayuki, Masayuki and Yoshiyuki) and daughter (Kimiko) came to her home almost every day to play with the Furuta children.

During the early 1900s, there were numerous *Nihonmachi* (Japan streets or Japan towns) on the West Coast, most larger than the one in Wintersburg Village. The Tashima Market served the surrounding countryside, providing a meeting point for both the Japanese and other farmers from around Orange County.

Masako Tashima seems to have loved Wintersburg, where the family set down roots. Her children most likely attended the Ocean View Grammar School and Huntington Beach High School (archival information for the Colorado River Relocation Center indicates Masako's sons Masayuki and Takayuki attended Huntington Beach High School).

While their friends, the Furutas, helped support the Japanese Presbyterian Mission, the Tashimas supported the first Buddhist church. In his 1988 oral history, Clarence Nishizu recalls the Tashimas providing the second floor above the market for Sunday school and services for the local Buddhist community.

"Mr. Tashima was an outgoing man and he was quite a leader in the community, taking part in organizing *Seinen Kai*, Young Men's Club," remembered Nishizu, explaining the Tashima Market's central role in the county's Japanese community.

"Around 1915 or so, [Tashima] built a two-story building with a grocery store on the first floor and a hall for social gatherings…The second story above the Tashima store was used by the community as a meeting place," Nishizu continued. "Since there were many young *Issei* in the area at that time, every year at the end of the year before New Year's, the *Seinin Kai* held what is called *Bonen Kai*, which consists of singing, Japanese plays, samurai dancing called *Kembu*, et cetera, to commemorate the sending off and forgetting the old year."

> *Pat Tashima: "What was Orange County like back in the early 1900s?"*
> *Masako Tashima: "Oh, very good. Quiet. And all my children born in Wintersburg, same place. They live there, go to school, so I like it there very much."*
> *Pat Tashima: "How were you treated by the different people?"*
> *Masako Tashima: "Well, all nationalities very good friends to me. Come every day and every night and speak with me. I was so happy."*

Masako raised six children in Wintersburg, surviving a round of typhoid and the Great Depression. Wintersburg established itself as an agricultural center for the county and a social center for the Japanese community.

After working and raising their children in Wintersburg, the Tashimas moved their market to the intersection of Beach Boulevard and Garden Grove Boulevard, in the city of Garden Grove. They were living in Garden Grove at the time of Pearl Harbor.

PEARL HARBOR, DETENTION AND EVACUATION

Pat Tashima: "Do you remember what you were doing when you heard about the bombing of Pearl Harbor?"
Masako Tashima: "Yes, 1941, morning around seven o'clock. We heard radio. My goodness. All of us standing up, 'What happened?' All children speaking, I feel so upside-down. I don't know what to say. So shaking, shaking."

Masako recalled the days afterward, when no one was allowed to travel more than five miles from their home, the early evening curfew and that all lights must be turned off at night. She told her granddaughter she was scared "most of the time" and stayed home. If she went out, it was fast, and she returned home as quickly as possible.

By May 1942, the orders for evacuation had come. Masako packed "one bag to put in clothes, and one plate each to eat; cup, knife, spoon, fork, that's all." Masako said she was "so scared, I don't know where I am going...Get on train, close windows, don't speak nothing, just few words."

Masako's husband, Gunjiro, had already been picked up by the FBI and taken to the Tuna Canyon Detention Station at Tajunga—the former La Tuna Camp operated by the Civilian Conservation Corps—outside Los Angeles. Those taken to Tuna Canyon included teachers, clergy of all faiths, judo instructors and those involved with language schools or Japanese associations. In 2006, *Rafu Shimpo*, the *Los Angeles Japanese Daily News*, reported that documents released by the National Archives in Laguna Niguel reveal the breakdown of the detainees as 2,316 Japanese, 131 German, 99 Italian, 2 Austrian, 2 French, 1 Polish, 1 Ukrainian, 1 Russian, 1 Dutch, 8 unknown.

The detainees were not allowed within ten feet of the fence but were allowed two visits a week with a fence separating the detainees from the visitors. The diary of one detainee recalls it was almost more demoralizing to have visitors, since the visits were only for thirty minutes and visitors talked with detainees through chain link, reaching their fingers through to make contact.

In 1991, federal archivists discovered Los Angeles–area detainee files, including over 2,500 individual case files for Tajunga and a relatively unknown U.S. Army–run detention facility in Griffith Park.

CIVIC INVOLVEMENT RAISED PROFILES

Masako recalls her husband "went with reverends, schoolteachers, professors, and doctors—that kind of people. They moved them all over without knowing where they were going." Masako believed he was taken because Gunjiro had been involved with the Smeltzer Japanese Association and other Japanese community organizations when they lived in Wintersburg.

During the association's years of activity between 1905 and 1940, Gunjiro Tashima is one of the men documented as serving as president, as was his neighbor, Charles Mitsuji Furuta; Wintersburg and Smeltzer labor camp manager Tsuneji Chino; and Wintersburg Japanese Presbyterian Mission charter member and elder Kyutaro Ishii.

Masako and her children managed to see Gunjiro before he was moved to a U.S. Army detention center in Lordsburg, New Mexico. She was worried that he was ill (Gunjiro suffered from Parkinson's disease). Recognizing the confusion and rumors of the time, he reassured Masako that "he didn't do any bad thing so, straight honest. [He] said, 'Ask me, I want to answer.'"

During the 1974 oral history interview, it was explained that Gunjiro "went willingly because he was taken. But he didn't do anything wrong…And had they asked him, he would have answered right away. Since he was never asked, he could never state his side."

Gunjiro later was moved from New Mexico to Arizona's Colorado River Relocation Center to join his family.

EVACUATION FROM HUNTINGTON BEACH

Those evacuated from Wintersburg and around Orange County gathered with other *Issei* and *Nisei* at the Pacific Electric Railway station in Huntington

Beach. Evacuees were expected to make their own way to the station. Arriving early in the morning, the evacuees were then put on buses for the daylong trip to the Colorado River Relocation Center at Poston, Arizona.

Hitoshi Nitta of Santa Ana remembers people were designated to arrive at the Huntington Beach station on different days. During his 1966 oral history interview, Hitoshi recalls there were "well over ten buses" on the day he evacuated. The regulations and notices for evacuation were posted on Southern California Edison light poles.

Nitta recalls there were Caucasians who were vocal in their opposition to the evacuation and that a group "served coffee and donuts to the evacuees the morning that we departed" from the Huntington Beach station. Henry Kanegae, also interviewed in 1966, remembered Baptist ladies from west Orange County serving coffee: "After I arrived at camp, I wrote them a letter thanking them for it."

The Nittas put their farm into the hands of their Mexican American foreman, who operated the farm and sold the produce for them. He visited them at Poston regularly. At the time of Hitoshi Nitta's interview in 1966, the foreman was still with the Nitta family at their farm in Santa Ana.

ENDURING POSTON

Masako reacted like most Japanese regarding Poston: it was nothing but sand—in their shoes, in the food, in the barracks, everywhere. "It was bleak," agreed Hitoshi Nitta. The use of green lumber in barracks construction meant barrack walls dried and shrank in Arizona's dry heat, leaving gaps through which sand continually entered living quarters.

The Tashimas' second oldest son, Noriyuki, had been drafted into the U.S. Army prior to Pearl Harbor. He was later awarded a Purple Heart after being wounded in France. Masako notes Noriyuki spoke three languages and later served as the first Japanese postmaster in the mainland United States, appointed by President Kennedy.

Nori's brothers, Takayuki, Masayuki and Yoshiyuki, later also served in the U.S. Army. At one point, four of Masako's sons were serving the U.S. military in different parts of the world.

RETURNING TO ORANGE COUNTY

After World War II and the confinement years, most of the Japanese markets and stores disappeared from Wintersburg and Huntington Beach.

Yukiko Furuta tried to remember the fate of the Japanese market owners during her 1982 oral history interview: "Mr. and Mrs. Oda, came back after the war and started the barbershop again. But Mr. Gunjiro Tajima who owned the grocery shop went to Cleveland after getting out of camp and didn't come back. [Gunjiro passed away from Parkinson's disease in 1959.] The other grocery store in Talbert had been run by Mr. Gizo Noguchi, but he also didn't come back here after the war, so there were no Japanese grocery stores in Orange County after the war anymore."

Eventually—although they did spend time in Cleveland—most of the Tashima family did return to California, according to the grandson of Gunjiro and Masako Eugene Tashima, who holds a master's degree in Asian American studies from the University of California–Los Angeles and, as of 2013, teaches sociology at Victor Valley Community College in Victorville, California.

Pool hall run by Ichibei Okamoto in Santa Ana, California, circa 1915. *California State University Fullerton, Center for Oral and Public History, PJA 389.*

"Masayuki and Kimiko settled in Cleveland permanently. The rest of the family eventually moved back to California. Hiroyuki and his wife, Mary, settled in the Crenshaw area. Gunjiro and Masako lived with them in the Crenshaw area," explains Eugene. "Hiroyuki eventually moved to Monterey Park. Noriyuki and Takayuki married sisters [Janet and Frances Tsuchiya] and settled in their hometown, Livingston, CA. After serving in the Army and graduating UC Davis, my other uncle, Yoshiyuki and his wife, Mary settled in Buena Park."

> *Pat Tashima: "Did you think it was kind of unfair?"*
> *Masako Tashima: "Well, I can't tell how. Fate is so mixed-up sometime. Everything change quietly."*
> *Pat Tashima: "As you look back, how do you view your whole experience?"*
> *Masako Tashima: "Well, not very sure. I don't like war. So many people sorry."*
> *Pat Tashima: "Grandma, were your feelings ever divided between Japan and America?"*
> *Masako Tashima: "Well, I lived in Japan so long, but I am so glad stay here. Of course, in Japan is all right—beautiful, I like. But if I want to stay, my life be in America. This is my country, so warm feeling."*

Chapter 15

RISING FROM CONFINEMENT

The Wintersburg Japanese Presbyterian Mission and Church provided guidance during the assimilation into American culture, strength during the traumatic World War II years and inspiration for higher achievement.

Among the congregants of national note is James Kanno, the first Japanese American mayor of a mainland U.S. city and the first mayor of Fountain Valley, California. Maki Kanno, his mother, was interviewed in 1983 for the Orange County Japanese American Project.

MAKI AND SHUJI KANNO

Maki Kanno's family was from the village of Toyano, Japan, now part of present-day Fukushima. Born in 1898, Maki Kanno was part of a samurai family, and her father was a large landholder, growing rice and silkworms. As a young woman, Maki went to nursing school in Fukushima and then later studied midwifery in Tokyo. During her time as a midwife, Maki helped deliver children of some of Japan's nobility.

Her future husband, Shuji Kanno, had left for America in 1904. When he returned to Japan in 1923 to marry his wife, he was thirty-four. They had never met.

Maki recalls Shuji had "came back to his village, *Akaza*...and it's a very small village, so everybody knew a man thirty-four years old, single, a man is here," laughed Maki, "and a twenty-five year old 'old maid' is in this village."

Describing herself as a "liberated woman," Maki borrowed a wedding kimono for the Japanese country wedding ceremony, but she skipped the traditional elaborate wig to simplify things. Maki's new husband, Shuji, liked her style.

The Kannos made the two-week journey by sea on the *Taiheiyo Maru*. Maki told

Shuji Kanno, father of James Kanno, first mayor of Fountain Valley, at his farm in Talbert. *University of California Berkeley, Bancroft Library, Hikaru Iwasaki, September 12, 1945, WRA no. K-278.*

her interviewer that her husband "was very sweet. Because she was afraid of being seasick, he chose a big ship and paid second-class fare for her."

When she arrived in the United States, it was Easter 1924. Shuji was already Christian, and upon their arrival in San Francisco, Maki was baptized. Like many new Japanese wives, she arrived in a kimono and immediately went shopping for Western clothes. She remembered the outfit during her interview almost sixty years later: "a blouse and a gathered light brown skirt."

Maki was impressed with her new husband. "A lot of the Japanese men told many lies in front of the brides-to-be, so they dreamed a big dream," she explained in her 1983 interview, "but when they arrived here, they found a tiny house awaiting them. Mr. Kanno, though, didn't tell her anything false."

The Kannos traveled by train from San Francisco to Orange County, to Shuji's ranch in Greenville, now part of present-day Santa Ana. Shuji Kanno leased acreage from German American Antone Borchard and grew asparagus. The Kannos lived on the Greenville ranch for fifteen years, and their sons, George and James, were born there, in 1924 and 1925, respectively.

A Wintersburg Japanese Presbyterian Mission Sunday school group in Wintersburg Village, 1926. *California State University Fullerton, Center for Oral and Public History, PJA 032.*

MEMORIES OF WINTERSBURG JAPANESE PRESBYTERIAN CHURCH

Maki Kanno remembered the Smeltzer Japanese Association in present-day Huntington Beach but said she preferred her involvement with the Wintersburg Japanese Presbyterian Church. Traveling from his asparagus farm in Greenville, Shuji attended night school at the Wintersburg Japanese Presbyterian Church before getting married in order to learn English. He eventually became an elder with the church and taught in a Saturday Japanese language school supported by the Wintersburg Mission in Costa Mesa, California.

Maki recalled Reverend Junzo Nakamura visiting "house after house…when Reverend Nakamura saw somebody working on their farm, he just walked over and talked with them. He didn't mind if his shoes became dirty."

"Mrs. Nakamura was a very, very nice person," said Maki, "She didn't have her own children, but she would baby-sit the other people's children. When there was a problem she was ready to help them. Both Reverend and Mrs. Nakamura were the center of the Japanese community. In that way, the church expanded."

Maki explained the importance of the Wintersburg church to her family. Shuji "was a Christian and he had a family, and he thought that to educate their sons in that Christian atmosphere was very important, so the Kanno boys were sent to the Sunday school classes at the church."

In addition to regular school during the week and Sunday at the Wintersburg church, the Kanno boys also attended the Saturday Japanese school where their father taught. During her 1983 interview, Maki told the interviewer, laughing, that her sons "are still very nice boys." By then, George was fifty-nine and James, fifty-eight.

EVACUATION AND INTERNMENT

Both George and James Kanno were interviewed as part of the Orange County Japanese American Project. They revealed in their interviews that it was probably their father's part-time teaching work at the Wintersburg Mission's Japanese language school in Costa Mesa that led to him being picked up as part of an early sweep of Japanese community leaders by the FBI after the attack on Pearl Harbor.

Japanese schoolteachers, landowners, judo club owners and members of local Japanese associations were among the first taken by the FBI. Among those picked up in Wintersburg Village were landowners Charles Furuta and Tsurumatsu "T.M." Asari, both crop and goldfish farmers. Furuta had lived in the United States for forty-one years and Asari longer, having arrived in America before the turn of the century.

Shuji was first taken to the Orange County jail and then to the U.S. Army's Lordsburg Alien Enemy Internment Center in New Mexico, while his family was taken to the Colorado River Relocation Center at Poston, Arizona. By then, Shuji had been in the United States for thirty-eight years.

In a *Los Angeles Times* interview in 1988, James Kanno told reporter Santiago O'Donnell he was "plowing land on May 12, 1942, when F.B.I. agents and sheriff's deputies pulled up in a car and made the arrests." The future mayor of Fountain Valley, James was fifteen years old at the time.

While there is no mention of it in the Kanno oral history interviews, the conditions at and the management of the Lordsburg camp were troubling. The New Mexico Office of the State Historian explains that "a protecting third power, in this case Spain, enforced the provisions [of the Geneva Convention]. During their tenure at Lordsburg, Japanese prisoners appealed to Spain saying that they were being mistreated."

The Pacific Electric Railway station was moved in 1941 from the Huntington Beach pier to Lake Street. Most Japanese living in the Wintersburg Village and Huntington Beach area were directed to gather at this station prior to evacuation. *City of Huntington Beach archives.*

Escalating tensions led to a camp guard shooting two Japanese in July 1942, during the time when Shuji Kanno would have been at Lordsburg.

When Maki, George and James Kanno were evacuated, they were taken to Huntington Beach with other local Japanese Americans to gather at the Pacific Electric Railway station and then, by bus, to the desert near Poston, Arizona. They leased their asparagus farm to a neighbor, who returned the farm to the Kannos when they came back to Orange County.

Shuji was detained at Lordsburg for one year before being reunited with his family at Poston. Maki told the oral history interviewer that she called upon her samurai resolve to get through that period, telling herself "this is a war" and that "as long as both of them were healthy, they would just have to wait and see…she believed in the government of the United States; the government would not do anything bad to them."

GEORGE KANNO

During internment, seventeen-year-old George Kanno took a work furlough allowed for internees, thinning sugar beets in Colorado. During his oral history interview in 1966, he describes the predominantly German farming community of Fort Morgan as welcoming to the Japanese.

"They understood our position because they were in Colorado during World War I, you see," explained George. "The Germans were treated pretty rough during that war, and they were real understanding of our predicament, and we got along fine."

"They had four churches in Fort Morgan that conducted services in the German language. They conducted services in German, and also in English for the younger generation who was raised there," laughed George during his interview. "So in several respects, they were similar to the Japanese. Certain things fit, you see, so they were better able to understand our position."

George Kanno later enlisted in the U.S. Army, sustaining a gunshot wound in his leg while guarding a supply train in Europe. When the Kannos sold their farmland, George became part owner of the Frontier Hotel in Las Vegas and the Sierra Produce Company, the largest produce supplier for hotels and casinos in Las Vegas.

James was still in high school prior to evacuation. The Kanno family was farming in Talbert (present-day Fountain Valley). Interviewed by the *Huntington Beach Independent* in 1999, he recalled "debating in his high school civics class that the Japanese evacuation would never take place because of America's democratic values." Three months later, Kanno and his family were evacuated and confined.

James graduated from the high school at the Poston camp—although hospitalized for a year with "valley fever"—and then was allowed to go to Marquette University in Milwaukee, Wisconsin. When the family returned to Orange County, James attended Santa Ana College and then the University of California–Los Angeles, while helping with the family's farm in Talbert.

Interviewed in 1971, James described his reaction when asked about internment: "My idea was that there were many people on the outside that realized that the evacuation was wrong, and because of the war and hysteria, through economic pressures and some other things, this evacuation came about. But a good example was the *Santa Ana Register*, the newspaper in Santa Ana [now *Orange County Register*]. Editorially the owner, Mr. R.C. Hoiles, indicated that this evacuation was wrong."

CREATING A CITY

In 1956—after receiving an engineering degree from UCLA while continuing to help the family's growing farm holdings—James was asked to serve on the committee to incorporate the Talbert area farmland into a new city.

He recalls, "People were starting to come into that area, and trying to develop it: buying up some of the property and putting it into housing, commercial and industrial uses. Several of the farmers got together and decided that for our own protection it might be a good idea to incorporate that area and form a city."

James was urged on by his wife, Fran: "I attended several of their meetings, prompted by my wife, who kept insisting, 'Gee, we've got property here, so you better attend those meetings.'"

The incorporation of Fountain Valley became a reality in 1957. James explained that "the two questions that were asked on the ballot: 1. Do you want to form a city, yes or no? 2. If so, who would you want as councilmen for the city? There were nine people running for the five council positions. I don't know what happened, but I ended up with the most votes."

James Kanno had become the first Japanese American mayor in a mainland United States city and the first mayor of Fountain Valley.

Jim Kanno's election and subsequent appointment as mayor made news around the world. *Voice of America, U.S. News and World Report* and Japanese media were among the news outlets that descended on the once quiet farming community.

"The '*Voice of America*' radio show heard about this and they came over to see me," recalled James. "In fact, they asked me to cut a tape interview with them, and I said, 'Well, gee, this is just a small farming community, and it's really nothing.' But they said, 'We're not asking you whether you will or not; we're more or less telling you to do so.' I said, "Well, gee, how come?"

The 1995 *Orange County Almanac* noted that "one Tokyo magazine pointed out that Kanno was elected despite the city's modest Japanese American population. The magazine said Kanno's election 'proves that there is still room for success in America.'"

With James's assistance, the young community of Fountain Valley developed zoning standards and built the infrastructure that made farming land more valuable for investors. Having increased the family's land holdings, the Kannos—like many of Orange County's farm families—eventually sold or traded land for other investments.

The *Los Angeles Times* reported in 1987 that James had acquired the Buffum's Department Store in the Westminster Mall, a Ferrell's Jr. ice cream parlor, a Bank of America branch building and a Carl's Jr. restaurant. James Kanno continued to manage his real estate investments, a result of his family's farming efforts, through retirement.

LOOKING BACK

James was philosophical about the experience of California's Japanese during his 1971 oral history interview, understanding the position taken by his father and other *Issei*.

Shuji Kanno had advised others detained at the Lordsburg camp who were preparing for their interrogations: "No matter what happens, America is where we came to and this is where we want to raise our children. So in spite of what happened, I feel that during this interview you better not say anything damaging, because we cast our lot. We came to America; this is where we want to raise our family; this is where we want to stay."

LOOKING FORWARD

James also relayed during his 1971 interview, a moment when his young son showed him the difference a generation makes. His son, David, planned to run for student body president at his high school:

"Why are you going to run for president instead of athletic commissioner or something like that?" He said, "Well, there are only three running for student body president, and the odds are better." So then I proceeded to tell him, "Well, David, we just moved into this area, and people really don't know you. Some of the kids went all through grammar school together, so they're well known.

"Besides, you have to remember, you're Japanese American and it might be a little tough to get in." Of course, I was the overly concerned parent; I was sort of preparing him for the defeat. But he said, "Well, Dad, you know because I am Japanese American, it's helpful." I said, "How's that?" And he said, "Because everybody notices me. I stick out. So that's how come I'm going to get elected and become president." So I said, "Okay."

Well, to make a long story short, he was elected student body president and was well accepted. So I guess sometimes we worry too much about the racial issue.

Chapter 16

THE BIRTH OF
ORANGE COUNTY

T he impact and influence of the Japanese pioneers in Orange County is becoming better known in the twenty-first century. In 2006–07, a project called *Preserving California's Japantowns* began surveys in communities throughout the state to identify the locations of Japantowns, or *Nihonmachis*, and what became of them. At that time, the extent of the community at the former Wintersburg Village was not well known, although the Furuta Gold Fish Farm and Wintersburg Japanese Presbyterian Mission complex was noted.

Charles Furuta (left) with unknown man in Wintersburg Village celery field, circa 1910s. *Furuta family collection.*

As of 2013, the Furuta farm and mission property are the last remaining features of the Japanese community in Wintersburg and the last remaining Japanese-owned pre–California Alien Land Law of 1913 property. The reach of the Wintersburg Japanese Presbyterian Mission was beyond Wintersburg Village, with Japanese language schools in Garden Grove, Talbert (Fountain Valley), Costa Mesa and Laguna Beach.

The Wintersburg Village became the heart of Orange County's Japanese community, due to the Smeltzer-Wintersburg siding of the Southern Pacific Railroad, the Tashima Market and McIntosh Meat House, the local Japanese association's meetings and events, the temporary meeting place of Orange County's first Buddhist church above the market and the services and social functions associated with the Wintersburg Mission.

Some of the known places that can be identified with the coastal Orange County Japanese community include the following.

CHARLES MITSUJI AND YUKIKO FURUTA GOLD FISH AND FLOWER FARM

The Furuta Gold Fish Farm is located at 7622 Warner Avenue, on the south side of the former Wintersburg Avenue at Nichols Lane. The three structures associated with the farm are the Furuta bungalow, constructed in 1912; the barn, believed to have been built around the same time or prior to the home; and the 1947 Furuta family home, constructed by Raymond Furuta for the expanding family. As of 2013, the Furuta farm property has been identified by several historical research firms and by the U.S. National Park Service and National Trust for Historic Preservation as potentially eligible for the National Register of Historic Places.

WINTERSBURG JAPANESE PRESBYTERIAN MISSION AND CHURCH

The mission complex is located on the northwest corner of the Furuta farm property. The complex includes three structures: the mission built in 1910, the manse (clergy home) built in 1910 and the Depression-era 1934 church, a Spanish Revival structure prominent on the corner of Warner Avenue and

Nichols Lane. The growing congregation moved in 1965, and the present-day church is now located in Santa Ana.

TASHIMA MARKET

The first Japanese market in Wintersburg was started by Tsurumatsu Asari around or before Yasumatsu Miyawaki opened the first Japanese market in Huntington Beach in 1907. The Tashima Market has been identified as on the north side of Warner Avenue and east of the railroad tracks, near what is now Lyndon Lane.

Asari was a crop and goldfish farmer in Wintersburg, a member of the county's first Buddhist church and a founding supporter of the Wintersburg Japanese Presbyterian Mission. Asari signed the 1904 document used for countywide fundraising to build the mission. Oral histories note the Buddhist community supported and contributed to the mission-building effort at Wintersburg and that the mission congregants later support the building effort of the Buddhist church.

This civic and interfaith community support continued when Gunjiro Tashima—who had started as a stock boy at the market—bought it from Asari. The second story above the Tashima store was used by the community as a meeting place and for the *Bonen Kai*, or New Year's, events, with singing, Japanese plays and samurai *kembu* performances.

SMELTZER JAPANESE ASSOCIATION

The local Japanese Association for coastal Orange County—despite the name—was located in Wintersburg Village and used a Huntington Beach post office address. The association met in the second floor of the Tashima Market and served the Japanese communities of Wintersburg, Smeltzer, Bolsa, Talbert, Garden Grove and surrounding areas.

The Japanese associations helped with local community issues, coordination of produce to market and civic and social activities. The annual picnics of the Smeltzer Japanese Association were held in Huntington Beach parks (at that time, likely Lake or Triangle Parks) and at the beach. The association also supported youth sports, with baseball, track and field,

Orange County Japanese baseball, Bonshichi Yoshimura and Masami Fujino, 1922.
California State University Fullerton, Center for Oral and Public History, PJA 188.

basketball and judo teams. Japanese associations became targeted suspect groups after Pearl Harbor, as organizations with *Issei* and *Nisei* involvement.

BASEBALL

Between 1925 and 1926, the Smeltzer Japanese Association formed an Athletic Club, its first sport being baseball. It was a youth sports team, in which most players were *Nisei* under the age of seventeen. Before this, the Orange County Japanese baseball teams were *Issei*, with coach Sei Ida (son-in-law of the Ida Tofu maker in Garden Grove). Clarence Nishizu recalled in his 1984 oral history that the "*Issei* players didn't have much of a baseball team; nevertheless, they had a sociable group."

The 1933 Orange County *Nisei* publication, *Echo*, describes the baseball field used for practice as next to the Tashima Market on Wintersburg Avenue, "just opposite the Japanese church." *Echo* explains that "through the courtesy of Mr. Tashima, the boys were able to use a room in his house for dressing."

The coach, Sam Sasahara, had mentor responsibilities much like any Huntington Beach coach today, as "the boys often strayed to the beaches and failed to appear on the grounds in time to practice." Among the teams they played were the Long Beach Young Men and the Stanton Mexican team, some of the games being held at the "home field" in Wintersburg Village.

JUDO AND KENDO

In 1929, a large judo and kendo hall was created in a warehouse owned by Kamenosuke Aoki at the Masami Sasaki chili pepper dehydrating cooperative on Beach Boulevard in Huntington Beach, just south of Wintersburg Village. The publication *Echo* describes the "new *judo-bu*"—also known as the Aoki Kendo Hall—outfitted with "showers, dressing room and a fine mat."

At the time *Echo* was published in 1933, it was reported that "there are about seventy students, both Japanese and American. These boys practicing diligently have made themselves well known in Orange County and Southern California. They have given many exhibitions at high schools, clubs, American Legion Posts, Fourth of July celebrations, Orange County Fair, and also at the Olympic Stadium as one of the gymnastic events of the Olympics."

All of the judo and kendo students who participated in the mass judo exhibition at the Tenth Olympiad in Los Angeles in 1932 received a medal. At the time of the Tenth Olympiad, Jigoro Kano, the founder of the sport

Orange County judo team, 1932 (performed at Tenth Olympiad in Los Angeles). *California State University Fullerton, Center for Oral and Public History, PJA 234.*

of *judo* in Japan in the 1880s, visited the Huntington Beach chili pepper warehouse *judo-bu*, giving his blessing for the Southern California Judo Society to become an official chapter of the main organization in Tokyo. Judo was included as an official Olympic sport in 1964.

JAPANESE FENCING CLUB

When Huntington Beach dedicated its $70,000 pier in June 1914 (rebuilt after being destroyed by a Pacific storm), part of the celebration—also featuring legendary surfer George Freeth—included a performance by the Japanese Fencing Club. The June 20, 1914 *Huntington Beach News* provides the June 20 calendar for the pier dedication ceremonies, with Japanese fencing and sword dance at 4:30 p.m., just before the band concert and pier "illumination." A reported twenty thousand people came to the event.

Reverend Kenji Kikuchi of the Wintersburg Japanese Presbyterian Mission—by then in San Diego County—belonged to one of the many

167

Japanese fencing clubs in Southern California, whose members were among the first questioned by the FBI after Pearl Harbor. The local Japanese Fencing Club maintained a post office address of Route 1, Box 100, in Huntington Beach.

ORANGE COUNTY BUDDHIST CHURCH

The first Buddhist church in rural Orange County started with meetings in people's homes and moved later to over the Tashima Market in Wintersburg Village.

The Orange County Buddhist church describes the early years, "Like many fellow countrymen in their adopted land, the early Japanese settling here near the turn of the century took up farming as a means of livelihood. They raised such crops as sugar beets, chili peppers, and celery. Later years saw an increase in truck farms which furnished a variety of fresh produce for the dinner tables of the southland." The historical summary notes an early supporter, goldfish farmer Tsurumatsu Asari, and explains that "from about 1920, *howakai* [dharma talk gatherings] were held in private homes with ministers coming from Los Angeles 40 miles away...Later, the services were held in a hall above a grocery store operated by Mr. and Mrs. Gunjiro Tashima of Wintersberg [*sic*]."

In May 1936, the church constructed a building on Bushard Avenue in Talbert (Fountain Valley) on land owned by Mr. and Mrs. Taikichi Kato. The Kato family still owns the land as of 2013. In the immediate vicinity (Talbert and Bushard Avenues), there was a blacksmith shop, the campsite of the Escalante Circus—which paraded down Wintersburg Avenue when it was in town—Talbert's first post office and a school, and about four hundred feet from the Buddhist church was the Country Church of Talbert, which today still stands as the All Saints Anglican Church.

With the evacuation of Japanese on the West Coast during World War II, the majority of the Buddhist temple's *sangha* (assembly) were incarcerated at the Colorado River Relocation Center at Poston, Arizona. The church building was reopened in 1946 as a hostel for returning Japanese Americans without a place to live.

Orange County's first Buddhist sangha spent its early years in Wintersburg and maintained a post office address of Route 1, Box 630-B, in Huntington Beach. The Buddhist church is now in Anaheim, California. There is a historical marker on Bushard Avenue in the former Talbert, which notes the location of the first Buddhist church.

THE PACIFIC GOLDFISH FARM

The Pacific Goldfish Farm started as an experimental goldfish pond on the Furuta farm at Warner Avenue and Nichols Lane in Wintersburg by Henry Kiyomi Akiyama and his brother-in-law, Charles Furuta. Akiyama, married to Yukiko Furuta's sister, Masuko, went on to develop more goldfish ponds in partnership at the Cole Ranch. The Cole Ranch was located in the area of present-day Ocean View High School in Huntington Beach, at Warner Avenue and Gothard Street.

After goldfish farming proved profitable, Akiyama acquired forty acres in present-day Westminster. The history of the Pacific Goldfish Farm is included on the official website for the City of Westminster. It is proclaimed "the world's largest goldfish farm…[and is located] where the Westminster Mall stands today" near Golden West Street and Bolsa Avenue.

ASARI GOLDFISH HATCHERY, INC.

The Tsurumatsu Asari Goldfish Hatchery, Inc., was located at 8741 Wintersburg Avenue in Huntington Beach. Asari is reportedly one of the first Japanese to have arrived in Orange County, in the late 1800s. He was instrumental in the support for the Wintersburg Mission at its founding in 1904 and in the development of the county's first Buddhist church. Asari supported a variety of community efforts, including funding the local Japanese community's first aviator, Koha Takeishi, with the formation of the Smeltzer Flying Company.

The Asari goldfish farm was located near the 405 Freeway juncture with Warner Avenue in Huntington Beach, and the land is now predominantly residential.

THE ROCK BOTTOM STORE

Yasumatsu Miyawaki opened the first Japanese market in Huntington Beach in 1912 in the Talbert-Leatherman Building. Built in partnership with Orange County pioneer Thomas Talbert in 1904, the Talbert-Leatherman Building's original plumbing was installed by the city's first plumber, L.E. Worthy. This building—which started as a feed store and housed the city's

Leonard Miyawaki, age thirteen, with a forty-seven-and-a-half-pound leopard shark, 1924. *California State University Fullerton, Center for Oral and Public History, PJA 027.*

first gasoline pump—remains the oldest wooden structure on Main Street in Huntington Beach, the Longboard Restaurant and Pub (217 Main Street).

Wintersburg Japanese Presbyterian Mission congregant Clarence Nishizu recalled of the store: "Mr. Miyawaki must have been a shrewd and prudent businessman because he named the store Rock Bottom Store—how much lower can you sell?"

The Miyawaki family also managed a store off Bushard Avenue in Talbert (Fountain Valley), the Sun Rise Co. In the rural countryside of 1900s Orange County, Miyawaki used to deliver groceries to the Japanese farms by horse and buggy. Yasumatsu Miyawaki's son, Leonard, was born in the house behind the Talbert grocery store in 1911. By 1915, the Miyawakis sold the Talbert store to the Kushino family, due to their concerns about what affect the influence of the farm laborers and poolroom crowd might have on their son, Leonard.

Along with Tsurumatsu Asari, Yasumatsu Miyawaki—owner of the Rock Bottom Store on Main Street in Huntington Beach and the Sun Rise Co. store in Talbert—was one of the founding signatories on the 1904 document used for countywide fundraising to build the Wintersburg Mission.

RAFU SHIMPO

The *Rafu Shimpo* remains today the oldest Japanese-English daily newspaper in Los Angeles, with over a century of history. The paper began in 1903 as a one-page, mimeographed Japanese-language newspaper, with branch offices in Orange County, including in Huntington Beach, where it maintained a post office box: Route 1, Box 629. Publisher H.T. Komai took over in 1922 and made the newspaper bilingual.

The Little Tokyo–based newspaper shut down in 1942. H.T. Komai arranged for the paper's rent to be paid during the war and hid the Japanese type under the floorboards. Returned to publication after World War II, the *Rafu Shimpo* continues to cover events in the Japanese American community.

JAPANESE SEWING SCHOOL

The Japanese sewing schools offered domestic arts instruction to girls along with English tutoring. The physical meeting location of the school is currently unknown, although many of the early sewing schools met in the Japanese language schools or in someone's home.

The Pacific Sewing School Branch maintained a post office address of Route 1, Box 616, in Huntington Beach.

IDA TOFU FACTORY

The first Ida Tofu Factory was located at the west end of the Garden Grove Japanese Language School property, off Sherman Street in Garden Grove, California. Kikumatsu Ida and his wife, Kumi, made fresh tofu daily and delivered it to Japanese farmers by horse and buggy. The tofu was submerged in cold water and, without refrigeration, was good only the same day it was made.

In 1923, the tofu factory burned down when the adjacent chili pepper dehydrator warehouses caught fire. The tofu factory was rebuilt that year, north of the Japanese school, or *gakuen*, with financial support from the Japanese community.

THE MUKAI NURSERY

The Mukai Nursery was located off Edwards Street, between Warner Avenue and Slater Avenue, in the area considered part of the former Wintersburg District. Today, there remains a "Mukai Court" near Edwards Street and Athena Drive in Huntington Beach.

Hitoshi Toru Mukai was born in Venice, California, in 1923. His family moved to Huntington Beach in 1926. Prior to his high school graduation, Toru and his family were sent to the Colorado River Relocation Center in Poston, Arizona. Toru graduated from Huntington Beach High School in 1942, with the assistance of his teachers and school administrators.

After the war, Toru and his family returned to Huntington Beach and resumed operating the Mukai Nursery. For most of his adult life, Toru—who passed away in March 2012—owned and operated Mukai Nursery with his wife, Sadako, and their daughters attended school in Huntington Beach. In its early years, Mukai Nursery maintained a post office address of Route 1, Box 450-B, in Huntington Beach.

Japanese Language Schools

There were four known Japanese language schools associated with the Wintersburg Mission, located in Garden Grove, Talbert (Fountain Valley), Costa Mesa and Laguna Beach.

The Garden Grove Language School—built in 1914—was located at 10771 Sherman Avenue near Main Street, where the west entrance to the Costco parking lot is as of 2013. The school—with an architectural structure almost identical to the Wintersburg Mission—was demolished despite preservation efforts in 1991, after city redevelopment officials identified the property for commercial use.

The Talbert Japanese Language School was located near present-day Bushard Street and Talbert Avenue in Fountain Valley, a short distance from where the Buddhist church was located on the Kato property. It opened in 1912, the same year Charles and Yukiko Furuta built their new home on Wintersburg Avenue. Today, the area is predominantly residential. One of the driving forces behind the Talbert *gakuen* was Isojiro Oka, for whom an elementary school in Huntington Beach is named.

The Isojiro Oka Elementary School shares this history of the Talbert *gakuen* founder: "Many local Japanese-American children attended the school after their regular school day and on weekends to learn about Japanese language, history, and culture. Members of the community appreciated his quiet wisdom and often sought his good advice…Mr. Oka was generous with what he had. Many times he donated his vegetables to the Huntington Beach schools his children attended."

The Costa Mesa Japanese Language School was founded in 1930 by Shuji Kanno, an elder in the Wintersburg Mission and the father of James Kanno, who became the first mayor of Fountain Valley. The first school building in Costa Mesa was rented from the public school district and was located northeast corner of Nineteenth Street and Harbor Boulevard. Later, a new school was built on a five-acre parcel donated by Fanny Bixby Spencer. The Costa Mesa *gakuen* was located on the west side of Whittier Avenue, between Eighteenth and Nineteenth Streets, in Costa Mesa. Today, the area is commercial properties and nearby the Whittier Elementary School.

The Laguna Beach Japanese Language School was initiated in 1929, when Reverend Kenji Kikuchi with the Wintersburg Mission asked farmer Shinichi Matsuyama to allow classes in his home. Yukiko Kikuchi, Reverend Kikuchi's wife, was one of the teachers. The Matsuyama house was used for classes on Saturdays and the Wintersburg Mission on Sundays.

In 1932, the Crystal Cove public school building was used by the Japanese language school and the Wintersburg Mission. In 1935, the south Orange County Japanese community constructed a new school building on a bluff above Crystal Cove, west of today's Pacific Coast Highway. During World War II, the empty building was used by the military and, in 1949, moved to Crystal Cove.

The Laguna Beach Japanese Language School building is now the only remaining historic *gakuen* and one of the rare features the public can view of Orange County's Japanese pioneers. It is Cottage No. 34, the cultural center at Crystal Cove State Park, which is listed on the National Register of Historic Places.

EPILOGUE

In *Echo*, the 1933 publication of the Young Men's Association (part of the Smeltzer Japanese Association), Noboru Tamura writes, "It has been just a generation ago when our father's heavy boots first trod the American soil; since then they have encountered innumerable hardships and difficulties. We, the young people of today, 'only know the half of it.'"

Noboru Tamura was the eldest brother of Stephen K. Tamura, who went on to become the first Japanese American attorney in Orange County and the first Japanese American supreme court justice for California. The Tamura family attended the mission in Wintersburg, and Noboru stayed home to help on the family farm so his brothers could go to college.

Also included in *Echo*, is an essay by Leonard T. Miyawaki, whose father owned the first Japanese market on Main Street in Huntington Beach and the Sun Rise market in Talbert and was one of the founders in 1904 for the Wintersburg Japanese Presbyterian Mission.

"When tomorrow arrives," writes Miyawaki, "will we be able to hear the music of long ago, music which will refresh our old hearts with the glorious days of youth...I make my plea to you with all my heart, O you Orange County young people, let us bind together for a life of faithfulness through the long years to come for a close and happy union at the end."

Orange County's Japanese pioneer heritage is a story about which we "only know the half" and whose "music of long ago" bears telling for future generations. Of the thirty-three buildings noted on the Orange County Japanese American Council's Historic Building Survey in 1986, very few remain. After more than a century, the tangible reminders that the Wintersburg Village and Orange County's pioneer Japanese community existed are disappearing from the urban landscape. As of the beginning of 2014, the six remaining historic structures of the Furuta farm and the Wintersburg Japanese Mission are slated for demolition.

THE KNOWN TIMELINE

Historic Wintersburg has its roots in the mid- to late 1800s, with the formation of Wintersburg Village in the peatlands. The rich farmland brought a diverse group of people from across the country and across the seas, all hoping to create a new life in California.

Huntington Beach party, circa 1933–35. *California State University Fullerton, Center for Oral and Public History, PJA 357.*

1893: Henry Winters promotes Orange County at the World's Columbian Exposition in Chicago. Winters was named president of the California Celery Company and helped place Orange County celery in eastern U.S. markets. Winters also donated land for the Southern Pacific Railroad line that went through Wintersburg. Residents circulated a petition to name the town in his honor, creating the little community of Wintersburg Village.

A great-granddaughter of Henry Winters, Diane Daly, writes to Historic Wintersburg in 2013, "He was born Luther Henry Winters, in Warren[, Ohio,] and married Cordelia Wilson, who was born in Pasadena. My mother and cousin, who are granddaughters of Henry, are still alive in [California]. They tell me that Henry's land was on Warner and Gothard. He had [six] children, my grandmother Bonnie was the oldest."

A 1920 "Huntington Beach–Newport Oil Fields" map shows Henry Winters owned property west of the Southern Pacific Railroad tracks near Gothard Avenue, north of Wintersburg Avenue, within a couple minutes' walking distance northwest of the Charles and Yukiko Furuta farm and Wintersburg Japanese Presbyterian Mission.

1900: Eighteen-year-old Charles Mitsuji Furuta arrives in America, first in Washington State. He is prevented from disembarking in Hawaii to join his brother, Soichi, due to bubonic plague and continues alone to America. He works in the lumber and railroad industry for a few years in Tacoma, Washington.

A mass meeting in San Francisco, California, to discuss the bubonic plague outbreak adopted a resolution that the Chinese Exclusion Act be extended to apply to the Japanese.

1901: The California legislature adopts its first resolution urging Congress to restrict Japanese immigration.

1902: Clergy begin walking into the celery fields in the Wintersburg area to talk with Japanese bachelor laborers. Labor camps are located off present-day Springdale Street and Warner Avenue and in the area of Smeltzer (north Huntington Beach). One of the camps is managed by Tsuneji Chino, one of the first Japanese to arrive in Orange County along with goldfish farmer Tsurumatsu Asari. Chino later becomes a good friend of Charles and Yukiko Furuta.

1904: Wintersburg Mission effort founded by Reverend Hisakichi Terasawa, a Cambridge-educated Episcopalian minister, with support from the Presbyterian community of nearby Westminster. The newly formed congregation begins meeting in a barn in Wintersburg Village. This coincides with a community meeting in the armory building in Wintersburg among Presbyterians and Methodist Evangelicals regarding the need for churches in the growing village.

The American Federation of Labor adopts a resolution at a San Francisco, California convention to exclude Japanese and Koreans, as well as Chinese laborers.

1905: In 1905, fireworks for the Fourth of July were donated by the "Japanese Association of Wintersburg," which put on the show in a downtown Huntington Beach baseball field. During the early years of the twentieth century, the Japanese community participated in Independence Day activities with wrestling matches and dance exhibitions and handled the fireworks display. In 1935, the Huntington Beach parade included full-fledged Japanese and Spanish divisions."

The California legislature passes a second resolution demanding Congress take action limiting the immigration of Japanese. The Asiatic Exclusion League was organized in San Francisco. The Los Angeles Chamber of Commerce goes on record opposing discrimination toward Japanese.

1906: The present-day Warner Avenue Baptist Church is constructed as the Wintersburg M.E. Church. Henry Winters donated the land for the church in 1906, and Wintersburg resident James Cain donated a house for the parsonage. A Cain Drive remains, south of the Warner Avenue Baptist Church (formerly the Wintersburg M.E. Church) off Gothard Avenue.

President Theodore Roosevelt denounces an order by the San Francisco school board to segregate the school system, excluding Japanese. Japan and the U.S. government enter the "Gentlemen's Agreement," under which the Japanese government agreed to limit passports.

1908: Land documents from the Orange County archives show the Furuta farm and Wintersburg Japanese Presbyterian Mission property was purchased this year, first by Reverend Terasawa, for a recorded ten dollars. The property was purchased by and deeded to Charles Furuta for ten dollars in 1912; he later donated land to the church.

The Great White Fleet sails into Yokohama Harbor in a show of friendship between the United States and Japan. As a result, California legislators introduce a series of bills to segregate Japanese immigrant children from the public school system. President Theodore Roosevelt wires California governor James Gillett protesting actions counter to national policy.

1909: Construction begins on the Wintersburg Japanese Presbyterian Mission. Huntington Beach incorporates in February.

Seventeen anti-Japanese bills are introduced in the California legislature, ranging from school segregation to publishing statistics about Japanese in the state.

1910: The Wintersburg Japanese Presbyterian Mission construction is completed, and the first services are held. The manse, then on the east side of the mission, is completed this year by builder J. Hori. Reverend Joseph K. Inazawa and his wife, the former Miss Kate Alice Goodman, take up residence in the manse.

Report published by state labor commissioner J.D. MacKenzie concludes Japanese labor is essential to California agriculture. MacKenzie's report states:

> *Japanese land owners are of the best class; they are steady and industrious, and from their earnings purchase land of low value and poor quality. The care lavished upon this land is remarkable, and frequently its acreage has increased several hundred percent in a year's time...Some form of labor such as is now represented by the Japanese is essential for the continuance and development of the specialized agricultural industry of California.*

The report is disapproved and suppressed by the State Senate.

1911: California Senate passes a bill prohibiting land ownership by aliens not eligible for citizenship, which dies in an assembly committee and with intervention from President William Howard Taft.

1912: The Wintersburg Japanese Presbyterian Mission supports the establishment of the Japanese Language School in Talbert (Fountain Valley).

Reverend Hisakichi Terasawa deeds the five acres in Wintersburg Village in title to Charles Furuta, including the president of the Japanese Mission Building Committee, for a recorded ten dollars.

Charles Mitsuji Furuta, thirty-one, travels back to Japan to meet his bride, Yukiko Yajima, seventeen. They return to America on the *Shinyo Maru* of the Toyo Kisen Kaisha ship line, later NYK (the Japan Mail Steamship Co.).

Yukiko Furuta and son Raymond on Cole Ranch in Wintersburg circa 1915. *California State University Fullerton, Center for Oral and Public History, PJA 309.*

1913: The final touches are made on the Furuta bungalow, freshly painted with red iron oxide and white trim. During her 1982 oral history interview, Yukiko Furuta explained, "It was originally about half the size of the present house, because only two people lived in it. It had a living room, a kitchen, and two bedrooms...There was no electricity, no city gas, and...an outdoor bathroom. The road in front of the house was so muddy that when it rained she couldn't walk on it."

Japanese pioneer aviator Koha Takeishi flies his Curtiss model airplane from Dominguez Hills airfield to Wintersburg. His plane was purchased through a fundraising effort by Smeltzer and Wintersburg farmers who raised $4,000 and formed the Smeltzer Flying Company. Takeishi is killed at an airshow in Osaka later this year.

President Woodrow Wilson sends a friendly message to Japan and dispatches Secretary of State William Jennings Bryan to California to plead against passage of the Alien Land Law as obstructing the treaty obligations of the United States. California governor Hiram Johnson signs the Alien Land Law of 1913 on May 19 (effective August 10), prohibiting aliens ineligible for citizenship from owning land but permitting leases lasting up to three years. Directed at the Japanese, the law also affected Chinese, Indian and Korean immigrants.

Dr. J. Soyeda of the Associated Chambers of Commerce of Japan visits the United States and publishes *Survey of the Japanese Question in California,* urging the Japanese and American cultures to attempt to understand each other. An editorial in the San Francisco *Examiner* derides Soyeda's efforts.

1914: The newly reconstructed Huntington Beach pier is dedicated, including daylong festivities that feature a demonstration by Hawaiian-Irish surfer George Freeth and a fencing and sword dance demonstration by the local Japanese community.

California congressman John Raker introduces a bill to exclude Japanese from the United States. The U.S. House of Representatives rejects the bill as not being in the national interest.

1916: The Japanese Language School opens in Garden Grove, California.

1917: The U.S. Congress passes the Immigration Act of 1917, overriding President Woodrow Wilson's veto. The act includes an Asiatic Barred Zone, including most of Asia and the Pacific Islands, from which people could not immigrate.

1918: The Spanish flu pandemic sweeps the world, causing over a half million deaths in the United States and killing nearly 6 percent of the world's population. According to Clarence Nishizu:

> *It was taken for granted that all members of every family would be afflicted by this flu. Our family was no exception. Every member of our family came down with the flu. I was only ten or so years old when this epidemic hit. One day we found out that my parents both had been infected, and that there was nobody to care for us. Suddenly, Mr. Goya came to our house. My mother asked him to please leave, or otherwise he would certainly contract the flu himself. But he utterly refused to go.*

1919: "Wintersburg Folk Join Celebration" is a headline on the September 12 *Santa Ana Register*, featuring an article about a reception for returning World War I soldiers. "The Wintersburg-Smeltzer section was well represented at the reception for soldiers and sailors at the Orange County Park Admission day, among which were numbers of local service men who have returned home." Among those at the event noted by the *Santa Ana Register* were the Gothards, the Worthys, the Grahams, Mr. and Mrs. Ray Moore, the Kettler family, the Nichols family and Reverend Junzo Nakamura of the Wintersburg Japanese Presbyterian Mission.

California legislature proposes Alien Land Law amendments, affecting diplomatic relations between the United States and Japan at the Paris Peace Conference.

1920: California passes the Alien Land Law of 1920, imposing additional restrictions to the 1913 law. Under the 1920 law, leasing land for a period of three years or less and owning stock in agricultural companies is prohibited. Those identified as agents or guardians of ineligible aliens are required to submit an annual report on their activities.

1922: The U.S. Congress passes the Cable Act, which strips citizenship of women who marry anyone ineligible for citizenship, applying solely to Asians who were prohibited from gaining citizenship.

1923: The U.S. Supreme Court upholds the California Alien Land Law, concluding it did not violate the equal protection and due process guaranties of the Fourteenth Amendment.

Huntington Beach City Council unanimously approves a $100 donation to the Japan Relief Fund within days of a devastating earthquake in Japan.

1924: Senator Samuel Shortridge of California succeeded in amending the Immigration Act of 1924 to permanently exclude Japanese from immigration to the United States.

1926: Reverend Kenji Kikuchi and family arrive in Wintersburg Village, replacing Reverend Junzo Nakamura, and take up residence in the manse. Reverend Kikuchi remains the clergy at Wintersburg Japanese Presbyterian

Chili peppers on drying racks at Bolsa, circa 1925. *California State University–Fullerton, Center for Oral and Public History, PJA 053.*

Mission during the time it organized as a church and built its second building in 1934, departing in 1936.

1929: Black Tuesday comes on October 29 and, with it, the Great Depression. Reverend Kenji Kikuchi of the Wintersburg Japanese Presbyterian Mission ran to the Huntington Beach Bank to find out what happened to the church funds. "We almost felt like crying," he remembered. "But, later, when we fixed pews in the church, we could draw our deposit from the bank after the arrangement by the government. In this way, we collected small amounts of money little by little."

The Wintersburg Japanese Presbyterian Mission helps start a Japanese Language School at Laguna Beach, first in the home of Shinichi Matsuyama, one of the local farmers. Matsuyama also opened his home for the Wintersburg Mission services. On Saturday, his house was open for language, and on Sunday, it was open for church service.

1930: Reverend Kenji Kikuchi reports on the "new Sunday school at Laguna Beach" in a typed history of the church, then writing it was one of the "oldest Japanese churches in Southern California." The mission officially becomes an organized Presbyterian Church, twenty-six years after its founding in 1904.

The Costa Mesa Japanese Language School opens at Whittier Avenue on land bequeathed to Tosh Ikeda by Fanny Bixby Spencer (the first Costa Mesa school building was leased from the school district and was at Nineteenth Street and Harbor Boulevard). The school is founded by Wintersburg Japanese Presbyterian Mission congregant Shuji Kanno, father of James Kanno, the first mayor of Fountain Valley and first Japanese American mayor of a continental U.S. city. The Wintersburg Japanese Presbyterian Mission supports the school, with classes taught by Reverend Sohei Kowta when he arrives in 1938.

1933: The sole edition of *Echo* is published by the American-born Nisei Young Men's Association in Orange County, with essays and accounts of life in the Japanese community as the second generation comes of age.

1934: The Wintersburg Japanese Presbyterian Church opens the doors to its new building, a classic southern California Spanish Revival style. The congregation managed to raise funds and build during the Great Depression, seeking funds from all over Orange County.

The original 1910 mission and manse remain on the property, now hidden from view by the 1934 church building. Behind the manse, the clergy kept chickens and other small livestock to feed their families.

1935: The Japanese Language School and Sunday services supported by the Wintersburg Japanese Presbyterian Church expand at the Laguna Beach location, with a new building built on the bluff above Crystal Cove. The school was used primarily for school purposes but also served as a multipurpose meeting center, with kendo, youth dances, Japanese culture, funerals, Buddhist and Christian services, an annual Christmas play and farm meetings. One mission congregant notes the community formed what may have been the first Japanese farm cooperative, purchasing seed as the Laguna Beach Growers' Association.

The building used for the Laguna Beach *gakuen* and community center is now Cottage No. 34, the cultural center at Crystal Cove State Park, which is on the National Register of Historic Places.

1938: Reverend Sohei Kowta and family begin living in the manse, while he serves the Wintersburg and Greater Orange County community. They continue to live in the manse until evacuated to the Colorado River Relocation Center in 1942.

Wintersburg Japanese Presbyterian Church congregant Stephen K. Tamura becomes the first Japanese American attorney in Orange County after attending Harvard University. His law practice opens at 202 East Fourth Street in Santa Ana. The law office building is one of the last Japanese American historical sites extant in Orange County today.

1941: Pearl Harbor.

1942: Executive Order 9066 is signed on February 19 by President Franklin D. Roosevelt. The order created military exclusion zones in the western United States and led to the forced evacuation and confinement of over 120,000 Americans of Japanese ancestry. Over 60 percent were American citizens, born in the United States.

The Furuta family and Reverend Kowta and family are evacuated and confined at the Colorado River Relocation Center. Charles Mitsuji Furuta is first taken to the Huntington Beach Jail, then to Tajunga's "Tuna Canyon" immigration detention center and finally to a military detention center at the Lordsburg Alien Internment Center in New Mexico. Within the same camp at Poston, Arizona, are the Furuta, the Akiyama and Kowta families.

The *Santa Ana Register* (now *Orange County Register*) runs an editorial by its owner, R.C. Hoiles, on October 14 regarding the forced evacuation and confinement of Japanese Americans:

> *The question we should consider is whether or not this evacuation will in the long run really help us win the war. If it will not, we should make every effort possible to correct the error as rapidly as possible. It would seem that convicting people of disloyalty to our country without having specific evidence against them is too foreign to our way of life and too close akin to the kind of government we are fighting. We need all the manpower we can obtain. To remove the Japanese from the place where they could serve our country by helping us furnish food and doing useful services weakens us in our defense by that amount. We must realize, as Henry Emerson Fosdick so wisely said, "Liberty is always dangerous but it is the safest thing we have." That, also, in reality, means that true democracy is always dangerous but it is the safest thing we have. If we are not willing to run any risks and cannot have faith in humanity and regard people innocent until they are proved guilty, we are on the road to losing our democracy.*

1945: The Furuta family return home to Wintersburg Village and begin to recover their farm. Reverend Sohei Kowta and family return to the Little Tokyo area of Los Angeles to help with the Union Church and Evergreen Hostel.

1952: Congress passes the Immigration and Nationality Act of 1952, which provides an opportunity for citizenship to residents of Asian ancestry, while restricting immigration from Eastern Europe.

1952–53: Charles Furuta passes U.S. citizenship class conducted at Huntington Beach High School, half a century after arriving in America.

1953: Charles Furuta passes away from cancer in October, before he has a chance to become a naturalized citizen. He had lived in the United States for fifty-three years.

1957: The Furuta farm and Wintersburg Japanese Presbyterian Mission complex are part of the annexation of Wintersburg Village to the City of Huntington Beach. Fountain Valley (formerly Talbert) incorporates. Wintersburg Japanese Presbyterian Mission congregant James Kanno—who had been incarcerated at the Colorado River Relocation Center as a teenager—is elected as the first mayor of Fountain Valley and becomes the first Japanese American mayor in a mainland city.

Kanno explained during his 1971 oral history interview that "the two questions that were asked on the ballot: 1. Do you want to form a city, yes or no? 2. If so, who would you want as councilmen for the city? There were nine people running for the five council positions. I don't know what happened, but I ended up with the most votes."

1961: Wintersburg Japanese Presbyterian Mission congregant Stephen K. Tamura becomes the first Japanese American appointed to the Orange County Superior Court. Reverend Kenji Kikuchi referred to him as "one of my Sunday school boys."

1965: Wintersburg Presbyterian Church relocates to a larger property on Fairview Street in Santa Ana.

1966: The National Historic Preservation Act is signed, creating the National Register for Historic Places.

Wintersburg Japanese Presbyterian Mission congregant Clarence Nishizu is the first Japanese American selected as foreman of the Orange County Grand Jury.

Wintersburg Japanese Presbyterian Mission congregant Stephen K. Tamura becomes the first Japanese American appellate judge in the continental United States.

1973: The City of Huntington Beach Open Space/Conservation report identifies "Old Japanese Church" as a historical cultural landmark.

1983: A Cultural Resource Survey Report for the Warner Avenue Widening and Reconstruction Project by Scientific Resource Surveys, Inc., recommends the Furuta farm and Wintersburg Japanese Mission property and its structures as potentially eligible for the National Register of Historic Places.

1986: A Historic Buildings Survey by the Bowers Museum Japanese American Council notes the Japanese Mission complex and Furuta farm property as number one on the list of important historical sites, noting "churches and schools served as focal points for small Japanese communities." The survey found thirty-three surviving buildings in 1986; most have vanished as of 2013.

The Huntington Beach Historic Resources Board includes the "Japanese church buildings" on their list of "high priority structures" for preservation.

1988: President Ronald Reagan signs the Civil Liberties Act of 1988, granting reparations to Japanese Americans forcibly evacuated and confined during World War II. During his official remarks at the signing, President Reagan specifically remembers the Masuda family of Talbert (Fountain Valley), congregants of the Wintersburg Japanese Presbyterian Mission. Another mission congregant, Clarence Nishizu, is at the signing, having actively supported the legislation.

1996: The City of Huntington Beach lists "Furuta House" and "Japanese Church" as local landmarks in its Historic Resources Cultural Element of City's General Plan.

2002: Greystone Homes plans multifamily residential development on Historic Wintersburg property but faces opposition from nearby Rainbow Disposal.

2004: Huntington Beach City Council rejects proposal to rezone the Historic Wintersburg property as commercial or industrial. Discussions are held with an affordable homebuilder. Rainbow Disposal purchases Historic Wintersburg property to prevent development.

2007: The Orange County Agricultural and Nikkei Heritage Museum at the Fullerton Arboretum opens its first exhibit, "Sowing Dreams, Cultivating Lives: Nikkei Farmers in Pre-World War II Orange County." A key force in the fundraising effort to build the Museum is Wintersburg Japanese Presbyterian Mission congregant Clarence Nishizu.

2009: The City of Huntington Beach marks its centennial anniversary. This also marks one hundred years since construction began on the Wintersburg Japanese Presbyterian Mission.

2011: City of Huntington Beach issues a Notice of Preparation for Draft Environmental Impact Report for the "Warner-Nichols" project of Rainbow Environmental Services (the former Rainbow Disposal), which proposes a zone change to industrial/commercial with an application for demolition of all structures. The demolition would include the Furuta 1912 and 1947 homes, the goldfish and flower farm barn and all three of the

Wintersburg Japanese Presbyterian Mission structures constructed between 1909 and 1934. The city's environmental assessment report for the proposed project notes all six structures as potentially eligible for the National Register of Historic Places.

2012: One hundred years since Charles Mitsuji Furuta returned to America with his new wife, Yukiko, upon their marriage in Japan.

2013: The U.S. secretary of the Interior announces a nationwide initiative with the U.S. National Park Service to undertake an Asian American Pacific Islander Theme Study to investigate the stories, places and people of Asian American and Pacific Island heritage. Ken Salazar says, "These are stories that will be part of the next chapter in our continued efforts to better tell the story of all of America and her people."

In a split vote, the Huntington Beach City Council on November 4 certified the Environmental Impact Report for the "Warner-Nichols" project, which rezones the Historic Wintersburg property to industrial/commercial and which approves the application for demolition of all six historic structures. The city council gives the Historic Wintersburg Preservation Task Force eighteen months to save the century-old Furuta Gold Fish Farm and Wintersburg Japanese Presbyterian Mission complex.

BIBLIOGRAPHY

"Analyzing a Future Husband." *Christian Work and the Evangelist* 88 (1910): 348.

Armor, Samuel. *History of Orange County, with Biographical Sketches.* Los Angeles, CA: Historic Record Company, 1921.

Atherton, Gertrude. *California: An Intimate History.* New York: Harper & Brothers Publishers, 1914.

Bolton, Herbert E., and Adams, Ephraim D. *California's Story.* Norwood, MA: Norwood Press, 1922.

Boscana, Geronimo, Alfred Robinson, Phil Townsend Hanna and John Peabody Harrington. *A Revised and Annotated Version of Alfred Robinson's Translation of Father Geronimo Boscana's Historical Account of the Belief, Usages, Customs and Extravagencies of the Indians of This Mission of San Juan Capistrano, Called the Acagchemem Tribe.* Santa Ana, CA: Fine Arts Press, 1933.

Chace, Paul. "Locating the Buck Ranch Prehistoric Burial Ground." *Pacific Coast Archaeology Society* 40, no. 2 (2008).

Cleland, Robert Glass. *California in Our Time, 1900–1940.* New York: Alfred A. Knopf, 1947.

———. *The Cattle on a Thousand Hills.* San Marino, CA: Huntington Library, 1969.

Daniels, Roger. *Prisoners without Trial: Japanese Americans in World War II.* New York: MacMillan, 2004.

Ferguson, Edwin E. "The California Alien Land Law and the Fourteenth Amendment." *California Law Review* 35, no. 1 (March 31, 1947).

George, Stephanie, and Carlota F. Haider. *Sowing Dreams, Cultivating Lives, Nikkei Farmers in Pre–World War II Orange County.* Tom & Chiz Miyawaki Legacy

Project, Orange County Agricultural and Nikkei Heritage Museum, Center for Oral and Public History, California State University–Fullerton, 2009.

Girdner, Audrie, and Anne Loftis. *The Great Betrayal: The Evacuation of Japanese-Americans During World War II*. London: MacMillan Company, Collier-MacMillan Ltd., 1969.

Graves, Jackson A. *California Memories, 1857–1930*. Los Angeles, CA: Times Mirror Press, 1930.

Gunji, Nao. "Community Unites to Save Former Japanese Site." *Rafu Shimpo–Los Angeles Japanese Daily News*, September 14, 2009.

Federal Bureau of Investigation. *Custodial Detention Japanese 1941*. File No. 100-2-60. Section 30.

Franklin D. Roosevelt Presidential Library and Museum. Japanese Internment: Collection of Documents Regarding World War II Treatment of Japanese Americans, 1941–1942.

Friis, Leo J. *Orange County through Four Centuries*. Santa Ana, CA: Pioneer Press, 1965.

Hansen, Debra Gold, and Mary P. Ryan. "Public Ceremony in a Private Culture: Orange County Celebrates the Fourth of July." Chap. 6 in *Postsuburban California: The Transformation of Orange County Since World War II*. Berkeley: University of California Press, 1991.

Henshaw, Henry Wetherbee. *Perforated Stones from California*. Washington, D.C.: Government Printing Office, 1887.

Hinch, Robin. "Determination Defied Defeats—Clarence Nishizu, 95, of Fullerton, Lost One Farm When He Was Forced into an Internment Camp and Another to Ill Health, but Went on to Become a Successful Real Estate Broker." *Orange County Register*, February 12, 2006.

Homyer, Lenora Marchant, and Maureen McClintock Rischard. *Pioneer Memories of the Santa Ana Valley*. Vol. 3. Santa Ana, CA: Ebell Society of the Santa Ana Valley, 1988.

Hunter, Allan A., and Gurney Binford. *The Sunday Before: Sermons by Pacific Coast Pastors of the Japanese Race on the Sunday before Evacuation to Assembly Centers*. Sunday Before Collection, GTU 97-5-02. Graduate Theological Union Archives, Berkeley, CA, 1945.

City of Huntington Beach. "Japan Relief Fund." City of Huntington Beach Public Records Archive, City Council Minutes, September 4, 1923.

Ikeda, James K. "A Brief History of Bubonic Plague in Hawaii." *Proceedings, Hawaiian Entomological Society* 25 (March 1, 1985).

Irwin, Charles. "A Material Representation of a Sacred Tradition." *Journal of California Anthropology* (1978).

Iwata, Masakazu. *Planted in Good Soil: The History of the Issei in United States Agriculture.* New York: Peter Lang Publishing, Inc., 1992.

Japanese American Citizens League. *An Unnoticed Struggle: A Concise History of Asian American Civil Rights Issues.* San Francisco, CA: Privately printed, 2008.

Johnston, A.J. *Final Report of the California World's Fair Commission.* Sacramento, CA: State Printing, 1894.

Johnston, Lonn. "Koi's Town: County's Akiyamas Have Been Raising 'Living Jewels' Since the 1920s." *Los Angeles Times,* January 27, 1989.

Kashima, Tetsuden. *Judgment without Trial: Japanese American Imprisonment During World War II.* Seattle: University of Washington Press, 2011.

Kikuchi, Reverend Kenji. "A Brief Report of the Presbyterian Mission of Wintersburg." Wintersburg Presbyterian Church, April 1, 1930.

Kling, Rob, Spencer Olin and Mark Poster. *Postsuburban California: The Transformation of Orange County Since World War II.* Berkeley: University of California Press, 1991.

Koerper, Henry C. "The Case of the Missing Buck Ranch Mortuary Remains: A Mystery Partly Solved." *Pacific Coast Archaeology Society* 41, no. 2–3 (2009).

Koerper, Henry C., and Nancy Anastasia Desautels-Wiley. "A Unique Artifact from the Dobkin Site, Unfinished Smoking Pipe, Manufacturing Die, or Shamanic 'Magic Trick.'" *Pacific Coast Archaeology Society.* 42, no. 2–3 (2009).

Koerper, Henry C., and Joe Cramer. "Additional Multi Holed Tablets from the Fred Aldrich Collection." *Pacific Coast Archaeology Society* 42, no. 2–3 (2009).

Kurutz, Gary. "The Only Safe and Sane Method...The Curtiss School of Aviation." *Journal of San Diego History, San Diego Historical Society Quarterly* 25, no. 1 (Winter 1979).

Library of Congress. Chronicling America. "Dr. Soyeda Sure That in the End California Situation Will Be Settled Amicably." *New York Times,* June 26, 1913.

Los Angeles Herald. "Celery Growers Elect Japanese as Directors." June 13, 1909, 7.

———. "Poolroom Robbed by Bandits." September 3, 1910.

Marquis, Neeta. "Interracial Amity in Los Angeles, Personal Observations on the Life of the Japanese in Los Angeles." *Independent* 75 (1913): 138.

McWilliams, Carey. "Once Again the 'Yellow Peril.'" *Nation,* June 26, 1935.

———. *Prejudice, Japanese Americans: Symbol of Racial Intolerance.* Boston: Little, Brown and Company, 1944.

Morgan, Warren F. *This Was…Mission Country, Orange County, California: The Reflections of Merle and Mabel Ramsey*. Laguna Beach, CA: Mission Printing Co., 1973.

Niedzielski, Rudi. "Oil Boom Recalled: Pioneer Writes of Huntington Era." *Daily Pilot*, December 15, 1971.

Nitobe, Inazo. *Bushido, the Soul of Japan*. New York, G.P. Putnam's Sons, 1905.

Platt, Tony. *Grave Matters: Excavating California's Buried Past*. Berkeley, CA: Heyday, 2011.

Quill Pen Club. *Rawhide and Orange Blossoms: Stories and Sketches of Early Orange County*. Santa Ana, CA: Pioneer Press, 1967.

Reid, Hugo. *The Indians of Los Angeles County: Hugo Reid's Letters of 1852*. Edited and annotated by Robert F. Heizer. California as I Saw It: First Person Narratives of California's Early Years, 1849–1900. Library of Congress.

Robertson, Georgia Day. *The Harvest of Hate*. Oral History Program, California State University, Fullerton, 1986.

Santa Ana Register. "Wintersburg Folk Join Celebration." September 12, 1919, front page.

Shippey, Lee. *It's an Old California Custom*. New York: Vanguard Press Inc., 1948.

Starr, Kevin. *Embattled Dreams: California in War and Peace, 1940–1950*. New York: Oxford University Press, 2002.

Strong, Edward Kellogg. *The Second-Generation Japanese Problem*. Stanford, CA: Stanford University Press, 1934.

Sturge, Dr. Ernest Adolphus. *The Spirit of Japan with Selected Poems and Addresses*. San Francisco, CA: Presbyterian Japanese Missions on the Coast, 1903.

Talbert, Thomas B., Mildred Yorba MacArthur and Don C. Meadows. *The Historical Volume and Reference Works Volume III Orange County*. Whittier, CA: Historical Publishers, 1963.

U.S. Census. Wintersburg Village and Huntington Beach Township Excluding Huntington Beach City, 1930.

U.S. Congress. *In Recognition of the Lifetime Commitment to the Community and Achievements of Clarence Iwao Nishizu. Congressional Record* 144, no. 25 (March 11, 1998).

U.S. House of Representatives. *Investigation of Un-American Propaganda Activities in the United States, Hearings Before a Special Committee on Un-American Activities*. 77th cong., 1st sess., H.Res. 282, February 28, 1942.

Young Men's Association. *Echo*. Orange County, CA: Young Men's Association, 1933.

ORAL HISTORY INTERVIEWS AND NOTES

Akiyama, Henry Kiyomi. *Issei Experience in Orange County, California.* Interview by Arthur A. Hansen and Yasko Gamo. Honorable Stephen K. Tamura Orange County Japanese American Oral History Project, Historical and Cultural Foundation of Orange County, Japanese American Council and California State University–Fullerton Oral History Program Japanese American Project, June 10 and 29 and July 27, 1982.

Chamness, Lee, Jr. *Japanese American Evacuation.* Interview by John Sprout, California State College, Fullerton, Japanese American Oral History Project, November 25, 1968.

Daly, Diane. Great-granddaughter of Luther Henry Winters, granddaughter of Bonnie Winters. Personal notes to the author. Historic Wintersburg, February 11, 2013.

Furuta, Etsuko. Interview by Professor Emeritus Arthur A. Hansen, Historic Wintersburg, 2013.

Furuta, Martha. Interview by Norman Furuta, 2005.

Furuta, Norman. Personal notes to and conversations with the author, Historic Wintersburg, 2011–2013.

Furuta, Yukiko. *Issei Experience in Orange County, California.* Interview by Arthur A. Hansen and Yasko Gamo. Honorable Stephen K. Tamura Orange County Japanese American Oral History Project, Historical and Cultural Foundation of Orange County, Japanese American Council and California State University–Fullerton Oral History Program Japanese American Project, June 17 and July 6, 1982.

Kanegae, Henry. Interview by Richard Curtiss, California State College–Fullerton, Japanese American Oral History Project, February 12, 1966.

Kanno, James. Interview by John McFarlane, California State College–Fullerton, Japanese American Oral History Project, April 26, 1971.

Kanno, Maki. *Issei Experience in Orange County, California.* Interview by Toni Rimel and Masako Hanada, Honorable Stephen K. Tamura Orange County Japanese American Oral History Project, Historical and Cultural Foundation of Orange County, Japanese American Council and California State University Fullerton Oral History Program Japanese American Project, November 30, 1983.

Kikuchi, Rev. Kenji. *Issei Experience in Orange County, California;* Interviewed by Arthur A. Hansen. Honorable Stephen K. Tamura Orange County Japanese American Oral History Project, Historical and Cultural Foundation of Orange County, Japanese American Council and

California State University–Fullerton Oral History Program Japanese American Project, August 26, 1981.

Kowta, Hiroko. Personal notes to the author, Historic Wintersburg, 2012.

Kowta, Makoto. Personal notes to the author, Historic Wintersburg, 2012.

Kowta, Tadashi. Personal notes to the author, Historic Wintersburg, 2012.

Nishizu, Clarence. *Nisei Experience in Orange County, California.* Interviewed by Arthur A. Hansen. Honorable Stephen K. Tamura Orange County Japanese American Oral History Project, Historical and Cultural Foundation of Orange County, Japanese American Council and California State University–Fullerton Oral History Program Japanese American Project, June 14, 1982.

Nitta, Hiroshi. Interview by Richard Curtiss, California State College–Fullerton Oral History Program, Japanese American Oral History Project, February 7, 1966.

Tashima, Eugene. Personal notes to the author, Historic Wintersburg, 2013.

Wintersburg Japanese Prebyterian Mission and Church historical documents.

INDEX

ABOUT THE AUTHOR

Mary Adams Urashima is a former journalist with thirty years of experience in media, government and public affairs consultation. Her work has involved local and regional governmental issues, environmental and land use projects and major infrastructure projects. She authors two local history blogs, Historic Wintersburg and Historic Huntington Beach, and chairs the community effort to preserve the property known as "Historic Wintersburg." Mary has received recognition for her civic work from congressional representatives, state legislators and local government agencies. She has served as a political appointee in the areas of regional transportation and municipal redevelopment and as a public official for infrastructure, human relations and historic preservation efforts. Mary also served as president of a chamber of commerce, as

a founding president of a multi-city senior citizen nutrition program, on the board of directors for a boys and girls club, on the board for an international humanitarian organization and on the board for a community volunteer center. She is one of ten Californians to receive the 2008 Civil Rights Leadership Award from the California Association of Human Relations Organizations and was recognized as one of the "Women Who Make a Difference" by the Orange County Community Forum. An advocate for historic preservation, Mary writes with the goal of furthering the understanding of America's diverse history and cultures. She lives in Huntington Beach, California.

Visit us at
www.historypress.net

....

This title is also available as an e-book

www.ingramcontent.com/pod-product-compliance
Lightning Source LLC
Chambersburg PA
CBHW060757100426
42813CB00004B/849